W.H. DAVIES: MAN AND POET

W.H. DAVIES
MAN AND POET

A Reassessment

MICHAEL CULLUP

Greenwich Exchange
London

Greenwich Exchange, London

First published in Great Britain in 2014
All rights reserved

Printed and bound by imprintdigital.net
Cover design by December Publications
Tel: 028 90 286559

Greenwich Exchange Website: www.greenex.co.uk

Cataloguing in Publication Data is available from the British Library

Cover art: © Mary Evans Picture Library

ISBN: 978-1-906075-88-0

CONTENTS

1

Contradictions

In 1895 or thereabouts, a young man of twenty-four years or so who had recently left Memphis in Tennessee found himself caught up in something of a riot. Memphis, now a commercial and industrial city was, even then, a busy place where young men went to find work in the port, on the railway, or in the relatively new industries which were fast growing in and around the city. Situated on the Mississippi river, it was an important trading and transport centre. Unable to find work there, and being of a restless and adventurous disposition, the young man had decided to make his way further south. His destination was New Orleans, and from there he intended to travel on to Texas.

The Southern States of the USA were then, as they are now, the home to large populations of black Americans. In the 1890s, most of them worked on the plantations and were little more than slaves, really. They were extremely poor and lived in simple wooden sheds, which were often delapidated and overcrowded. Sanitary conditions were extremely primitive and those who could find work were generally exploited by those they worked for. Disease, malnutrition and poverty made their lives barely tolerable, and crime, some of it violent, was relatively common.

The riot the young man witnessed was uncannily quiet. Armed white men were gathering in groups which tagged on to larger groups and, eventually, became one crowd of silent but angry men. This crowd of armed white men advanced along the main street of the town and made its way towards the town jail. Curious, the young man followed. He had some idea of the reasons for this sinister disturbance, and he wanted to see the outcome. A black man had recently been arrested for a despicable crime of some sort which the young man had been made aware of, and he suspected that frustrated anger among the white population was coming to a violent climax.

The crowd of armed men halted in front of the town jail and one or two of them banged on the door and demanded to see the sheriff. Almost immediately, the door opened and the sheriff appeared. After a short deliberation, the sheriff handed them the keys and several men entered the jail. Almost immediately, the young man heard a scream 'and a voice crying for mercy'. And then the men reappeared 'dragging after them a Negro at the end of a rope'.

In his account of what happened next, the young man vividly describes the black man's terror and his screams but, to the reader's surprise, shows no pity whatsoever. He can understand someone crying out in actual pain, but he has no sympathy for those who cry out in fear. The spectacle fills him 'more with disgust than pity'. He despises what he regards as the cowardice of a man who, unconcerned by the pain he has inflicted on his victims, is unprepared to accept his punishment.

When the black criminal is eventually strung up in a tree and summarily shot by the armed men who have dragged him from the jail, our young man is satisfied that justice has been done. And he later goes on to describe how he himself was physically assaulted and robbed by a gang of black men in New Orleans, reflecting that 'this not very intelligent race half murder a man without being sure of anything for their pains' whereas 'white men will search a man as he stands' and let him go if there is nothing valuable on his person.

Some years later, the same man was to write poem after poem about the sweetness and beauty of nature, the songs of birds, the simple pleasures of country life. Poems like 'Little Flower', which goes:

> Little flower, I hold you here,
> Between my finger tips;
> Can I do more for your sweet smell
> Than kiss you with my lips?

And so on. And so on, indeed, for poem after poem in a *Complete Poems* which comprises over seven hundred poems. What are we to make of this? And what are we to make of the man who wrote them: W.H. Davies?

We live in an age of biographies, an age which prides itself on its ability to come to terms with, analyse, and penetrate the characters of complex personalities, both famous and infamous, and these biographies often win national, and even international, acclaim for their authors. Whoever it is we are reading about, living or dead, we regularly allow ourselves to believe in the fictions which pass for their lives. And we are as confident in our judgements as those who have become our informers. We live, in fact, in a continous atmosphere of supposed enlightenment and clarification, and we are happy with the world such confidence reveals to us.

The truth, however, was never so simple, nor so gratifying. And in W.H. Davies we have someone who successfully managed to convince a whole generation of readers that he was a simple, loving soul who cared for nothing more than children, animals, his garden and such elementary pleasures as were open to all those who were prepared to believe in the simplicities of such an existence. But there is also evidence that he was unhappily trapped in the reputation with which the poetry-reading public had burdened him, although it isn't always easy to discover the truth in what Davies said about himself. He seems to have been constantly aware that anything he said could be easily misinterpreted and used against him. He was happy to inflate and exaggerate, when he was recounting his experiences as a tramp, but his deeper and more serious reflections he kept very close to his chest. Because he needed the money, he had to be careful not to offend those people who were either likely to read him or influence those who did. He guarded his reputation very carefully. His livelihood depended on it. However, there was another Davies, hidden from his more superficial and casual readers but buried, sometimes deep, in the huge corpus of mainly short lyrics which crowd the pages of his *Complete Poems*. That is the Davies we have to find.

There were few in the literary world, from John Masefield the Poet Laureate to George Bernard Shaw, who were unaware of his existence. In later years a plaque had been placed on the house in Newport, Wales, where he had been born and the university of Cardiff had awarded him an honorary Litt. D. And though never rich, he earned enough money from his writing to survive and eventually ended up in a pretty cottage in Nailsworth, a village near Stroud, in Gloucestershire. He died on 26th September 1940.

W.H. Davies left behind him a succession of literary works, both poetry and prose. They range from the prose accounts of his childhood, youth, and subsequent wanderings in the United States, to anthologies of verse. He published over fifty books in all. Apart from collections of his own poetry, he published selections from other poets, both living and dead. He even wrote part of an introduction to an edition of *Moll Flanders* and, as early as 1923, a tramp opera. He published two novels, as well. But most of his work was verse and, by 1940, when Jonathan Cape published his final *Collected Poems*, he had published well over thirty individual collections of his own poetry, punctuated from time to time with further *Collected Poems*. He was, predominantly, a poet and, although his prose is well worthy of study, it is as a poet that he would have wished to be judged.

So, what kind of a poet was he? And where, amongst the hundreds of poems available in his *Complete Poems* are we to find the true poet who survives the many contradictory impressions he gave of himself? Before we attempt to answer those questions, we need to learn more about his personal history and the events and circumstances which led to him becoming a poet.

2

Events and Circumstances

William Henry Davies was born on 20 April 1871, in Newport, in the present county of Gwent. At the age of three, he was adopted by his paternal grandparents. His grandfather, who was a retired Cornish sea-captain, was responsible for Davies's lifelong interest in the sea. His grandmother was a strict Baptist with puritanical views. Both were strong characters and their differences must have had something to do with the conflict between conservative propriety and unconventional individualism in Davies's personality. He was a curious combination of pride, shyness, guile, ambition and gentleness. Though he rebelled against the puritanism of his grandmother, he did so discreetly, and it was not until her death in 1893, when he was twenty-two, that he fully exploited the taste for adventure and travel which his late grandfather had stimulated. After having to leave school at the age of thirteen because of a series of gang thefts from local shops in which he had been involved, Davies worked for a few months for an ironmonger before becoming apprenticed to a picture-framer and gilder at the age of fourteen. He did not enjoy the work, and spent his leisure hours at the theatre or drinking with companions. What reading he did was mostly in popular novels, and his reading of poetry was confined more or less to the romantics like Byron and Shelley, though he did read some Shakespeare. He wrote a little poetry himself but published none of it, and was often restless. A few months after finishing his apprenticeship, he left his trade and went first to London and then to Bristol, living rough and, when his money ran out, relying on his grandmother to keep him in funds. He drank a great deal, kept late hours, and enjoyed an irresponsible and dissolute existence. He had no particular ambitions other than to savour whatever experiences came his way and, perhaps ultimately, go to sea. When his grandmother died, he saw his opportunity. The old lady had left him a legacy of ten shillings a week – quite a reasonable sum in those days – and this offered him the chance of the sort of independence he longed for. After securing an advance of £15 from his grandmother's executor, he sailed for America.

From this time began the series of tramping adventures chronicled principally in *The Autobiography of a Super Tramp* (hereafter called *The Autobiography*), which has become a minor classic. These adventures continued for a period of about six years, with periodic visits to England until, after losing a leg in an attempt to jump a train, Davies returned to England permanently. In the following six years, he wrote and attempted to publish a volume of poems in between periods of tramping and making a sort of semi-permanent base in a London doss-house. All this is described in *The Autobiography* and the account can be supplemented by reading Osbert Sitwell's introduction to the *Collected Poems* as well as the relevant parts of Richard Stonesifer's critical biography of the poet. Davies's first book, *The Soul's Destroyer*, was published in 1905, when he was thirty-four.

Davies himself had paid for the publication of his first book, prompted more by the need for fame than by any desire to see in print poems which had been created by any sort of internal pressure. That there were poems of that kind in the book, Edward Thomas was one of the first to realize. Fame, when it did come, came relatively easy to Davies and when he died the fame he had planned for had, indeed, become a reality.

His fame was in no small part due to the singlemindedness with which, in the months immediately following his first book, he courted the approval and support of well-known literary figures of the time. And, from those early days, Davies acquired a romantic reputation as a tramp-poet who wrote innocent nature-poems. Davies himself did nothing to discourage this view – and to some extent, actively encouraged it. His much anthologized set-pieces and his prose accounts of tramping and low life cumulatively distorted what was genuinely durable and important in his poetry. Though a relatively late starter, he had published five books of poems by the time he reached forty years of age. This was nearly equivalent to one book a year. His first *Collected Poems* was published five years later.

When Davies had to have his foot, and later part of his leg, amputated as a result of an accident caused while attempting to jump on a train in the United States, he was forced to accept that his tramping days were over. He was twenty-eight. Although he maintained, later, that he had always intended to be a poet, we cannot be sure whether or not this was the truth. Anyway, once back in Newport, while resting and considering what to do with the rest of his life, Davies tells us, in *The Autobiography*, that 'I pictured myself returning home, not with nuggets from the far West, but with literary fame, wrested from no less a place than the mighty London'.

Some time before his accident, while in Chicago, he read an article in one of the papers about Robert Burns and, he says, 'My thoughts wandered back to the past, to the ambition of my early days' (*The Autobiography*). We have no means of verifying this, and have to take his word for it, but certainly, once in London, he set about furthering his ambitions with a tenacity which was both courageous and extraordinary.

Apparently, he had already begun writing poems in Newport, prior to coming up to London, and had sent some of them to publishers. He received only rejections, and no encouragement. But London would be different. Having finally got himself a place at Rowton House, where he lived for the next two years, Davies was impressed by the library, which contained 'two large cases of books, one containing fiction, and the other being enriched by the poets, historians, essayists, with biography and miscellaneous literature.' Even at this early stage in his literary career, then, Davies perhaps imagined fame in a range of literature, rather than simply poetry.

He began by writing a blank-verse tragedy, entitled *The Robber*, hoping to have it produced on the London stage, but his attempt to sell it failed. Next, he tried a long poem, but he got nowhere with this, either. So he tried sonnets, writing more than a hundred at the rate of six or so a day. These, too, failed to attract the

attention of those he sent them to. Then he wrote a kind of
Elizabethan style tragedy, a comedy, and a volume of humorous
essays. Nothing came of them, and after a year no-one had
recognised whatever talent he had.

But he had accumulated a pile of shorter poems and began to
sense that he had some sort of talent for this kind of writing.
After a year of frenzied work, he began to develop a more practical,
critical sense of what he was capable of. He sifted through the
pile and picked out the poems which most impressed him, clipped
them together, and sent them to a few publishers in the hope that
they might be published as a single volume of his work. They
were rejected.

Davies did not despair, though. He chose three or four of the
very best of the selection and had them printed on single sheets
of paper. Two thousand sheets were printed for him, and he
hawked them from door to door. No-one was interested, and he
burnt the lot.

After two years without success, Davies was forced to move to
a Salvation Army hostel in Southwark. There was no library there
so Davies tried to work in local public libraries, but he found
himself unwelcome there and could not settle. So he had to work
as best he could, back at the Salvation Army hostel, in the crowded
kitchen. It was impossible. He had to leave the hostel and look
for somewhere more congenial. In the process, he ended up on
the road again, begging his way through the Midlands or trying
to sell pins, needles, buttons or whatever. Eventually, he ended
up in Stratford-on-Avon where, perhaps, the spirit of England's
greatest poet and playwright tempted him to return to London
and try his luck again. But he couldn't stand returning to the

Salvation Army hostel he had previously stayed in and was lucky enough to find a place at The Farmhouse, in Marshalsea Road. It was here that his literary career began in earnest.

In January 1904, when he was thirty-three, Davies once again began to send his poems out and the manager of The Farmhouse became aware of this. He had a word with Davies and told him that there was a possibility that he might be helped to publish his work through one of the charitable organisations that supported The Farmhouse. So Davies, encouraged by the manager's interest, prepared a collection of what he thought were his best poems.

Davies soon found a publisher interested in publishing his poems, for a fee. It was now necessary for the manager of The Farmhouse to find a sponsor. Sadly, no sponsor could be found and Davies, once again, had to live with this savage disappointment. But, although he spent many weeks harbouring his despair, he finally decided to start again with a completely new selection. This time he submitted the selection to Watt & Co, in May 1904. As had happened previously, publication was possible, but they needed a fee which Davies was unable to find.

He decided, in the end, to return to Newport and see if he could raise the fee from his grandmother's trustee, who was responsible for managing the small income which Davies received from his grandmother's legacy. He managed to get an agreement from the trustee, on condition that he received no income for the next six months. Davies, perhaps recklessly, agreed. He returned to London, determined to publish at all costs, but he could get no help at all from the manager of The Farmhouse so, taking his manuscript with him, he took to the road again, this time heading towards the west country and, after travelling much of the west country and returning via Guildford, Reading, and Uxbridge, he found himself once again back at The Farmhouse, in London. It was now December 1904.

In January, he got his money from the trustee in Newport, having survived six months of rough living, in virtual poverty. Immediately, he contacted Watts & Co. and arranged to have two hundred and fifty copies of his collection printed. He received the printed copies in March 1905. The collection was called *The Soul's Destroyer and Other Poems*.

Davies had, at last, begun his literary career.

3

Beginnings

The Soul's Destroyer was reviewed in two papers, one in Yorkshire and one in Scotland, but neither review was particularly encouraging. As far as the London papers were concerned, there was absolute silence. This time, Davies really was ready to give up his literary ambitions. All seemed hopeless. He was left with about two hundred copies of his unsold book, with no idea what to do with them. In the end, he stowed them away under his bed. Then he once again roamed the streets of London, in despair and often drunk. He even started to sing, and to recite his poems, in the streets just to make a few pence. His money was running out and he couldn't expect any more until he received his next six months' allowance.

Desperate, he studied the current *Who's Who* in a public library and drew up a list of important people to whom he could send copies of his book, in the hope of some kind of recognition. He sent the first six copies off, together with a letter of introduction, and waited expectantly for replies. Two sent back the price of the

book, and one referred him to a charity. There was a possibility
of getting some financial help if his case was deserving. Nothing
came of it but humiliation.

Davies consulted his list and sent off a dozen copies and four
were paid for. He sent out a further dozen. By the end of the
week, he had sold sixty copies. The money he accumulated enabled
him to survive financially. Just. And with one of the copies, he
was in luck. Sir John Adcock, who had influence with the *Daily
Mail*, recognised that the poems in the collection were not without
merit. He sent the price of the book to Davies and arranged a
meeting with him. But Adcock didn't turn up. Davies, however,
had already received two more favourable replies: one from Arthur
Symons and one from George Bernard Shaw. He once again
contacted Sir John Adcock and this time the meeting took place
as arranged. As a result, Adcock suggested he himself wrote an
article about Davies, describing his life and situation, for the *Daily
Mail*, and Davies agreed. Things immediately began to pick up.
He was featured in a literary journal, and Arthur Symons gave
him an encouraging notice. Consequently, Davies sold a few more
copies. Photographers appeared on the scene and Frances
Hodgson Burnett sent him an enthusiastic letter. More requests
for copies were received and visitors left their calling-cards at
The Farmhouse. Davies had become a literary curiosity. It was a
reputation which was to follow him for the rest of his life. Editors
who had previously taken no notice of his book began to request
further copies and photographs of Davies began to appear in the
newspapers. Davies was overwhelmed, and reviews of his book
appeared everywhere. Finally, he was approached by a literary
agent and his future was assured.

Davies enthusiastically began to get a further collection together. He was also visited by a poet who was to make a significant difference to his life: Edward Thomas. It was Thomas who wrote a singularly influential review of Davies's collection for the *Daily Chronicle*. And, as a result of Thomas's review and the reputation Davies had already acquired, Davies's agent, Pinkerton, encouraged him to concentrate on a prose book describing his tramping life which, Pinkerton was sure, would be very popular. And it was.

This book was *The Autobiography of a Super Tramp* and new literary friends, in addition to Edward Thomas, encouraged him in this enterprise. But, apart from various domestic problems, Davies was now becoming involved with the logistical problems common to all professional writers. He began to have trouble with his agent, and felt inclined to take over the business and promotional side of things himself. In the meantime, his domestic problems were solved by Edward Thomas, who managed to find him a little cottage near Sevenoaks, in Kent. Davies moved there in Febuary 1906. He was now thirty-five years old. But his new-found literary reputation was weakening. The newspapers had lost interest in him as a literary curiosity, and his agent was having less and less success with the publishers with whom he was in contact. In spite of the loyalty of his new literary friends, Edward Thomas and David Garnett, Davies was fast losing confidence.

But Thomas was an indefatigable help to Davies, both with his financial problems and with his professional ones. Garnett, too, read through the manuscript of *The Autobiography* and made detailed and helpful suggestions. And, from February through to August, Davies worked on the book. He also made the

acquaintance of, and, in some cases, friendship with, a number
of well-known writers: W.H. Hudson, Norman Douglas, H.M.
Tomlinson, Hilaire Belloc, John Galsworthy, Joseph Conrad, and
John Masefield, to mention only a few. And it was Thomas who
made this possible.

By March the following year, *The Autobiography* was still
unpublished, but *The Soul's Destroyer* came out in a second
edition, shorter than the first and more professionally edited. It
was published by Alston Rivers. In the same month, Elkin
Matthews published a second collection of Davies's poems,
entitled *New Poems*. Its publication was by no means as
sensational as the first, but the reviews were, without exception,
good.

Davies, however, was by no means financially secure. His
income from his books was very small. But an event was in process
of becoming which Davies hoped would give him financial
security and enable him to pursue his literary career with a
modicum of confidence. George Bernard Shaw, who had, for some
time, taken a keen interest in Davies, was writing a preface to the
coming publication of *The Autobiography*, in spite of some
anxiety about its effect on his own reputation. When his preface
was done, Shaw suggested alterations to the contract with
Duckworth which led to their disinclination to publish, and the
book was subsequently published by Fifield in 1908.

Strangely, the book was not as successful as one would have
thought. It certainly gave Davies a small but reliable annual
income for years, but it was not what we would call in modern
terms a 'bestseller'. It sold, and it sold steadily, and it did bring
his name and his extraordinary biography once again into

something of a spotlight. Readers from now on associated Davies's name with the kind of adventures recounted in the book, and he was able to exploit this interest with further books and articles about his life later on in his career. His poems, too, became accepted by various literary journals, American as well as British. And all the while, his poetic presence was acquiring the permanence which is necessary for literary success. Occasional publication also improved his finances, though never dramatically. He was still, to all intents and purposes, poor. But he lived simply and demanded little. His tastes were frugal and his appetites, except for alcohol perhaps, unsensational. He enjoyed the comforts of his small cottage, he enjoyed being known and having literary friends, and he enjoyed the privilege of being able to write and publish his books.

However, all this describes the superficial and practical aspects of his existence. Beneath his shy and secretive disposition there lurked a personality which felt haunted and fearful. He was never, in fact, psychologically secure. He genuinely doubted his talent, in spite of his apparent arrogance about his gifts as a poet. He was almost permanently anxious about something, whether it was money, or reputation, or the meaning of the dreams, and sometimes nightmares, he was prone to. He was abnormally sensitive, in spite of any impression he tried to give to the contrary.

But he had, at last, become an established writer and, among the rewards he was pleased to eventually receive, was a Civil List Pension of £50 a year for life. W.B. Yeats and Joseph Conrad were on the same list.

However, no writer's fame is perpetually ensured, whatever his or her immediate currency, and many of the names which were famous in Davies's day have since drifted from sight, their books gathering dust in library vaults or in dusty corners of antiquarian bookshops. Who now reads Ashley Gibson, Duncan Williams, Charles Dalmon, John Freeman, and Muirhead Bone? And the works of more significant talents, such as Ralph Hodgson and W.H. Hudson are more often than not out of print.

W.H. Davies, however, has lasted well. Although most of his books, in their original First Editions, are mostly sought after by collectors, his poems are still anthologised and reprinted fairly regularly, and books such as *The Autobiography* are relatively well-known. But the reasons for this are not necessarily obvious, and Davies has a reputation which, in some ways, distorts the true value of his work, both in poetry and prose.

It is time to explore these issues in more detail.

4

The Autobiography
of a Super Tramp

There is no doubt that *The Autobiography* is an extraordinary book. It bears witness, first of all, to a man's struggle against poverty and hardship, the courage such a struggle demands, and the adventures which are a necessary part of a life lived outside the customary boundaries of convention and routine. It is the first piece of substantial writing which Davies published and, some would say, has the kind of quality which has ensured its survival over more than a century. But what is this quality?

In introducing the very first publication of the book, George Bernard Shaw wrote that the book had 'that pleasant combination of childish freshness with scrupulous literary consciousness only possible to people for whom speech, spoken or written, but especially written, is still a feat to be admired and shewn off for its own sake'. In other words, Shaw was emphasizing the self-consciousness of Davies's written style, but what, exactly, might he have meant? When Davies had sent Shaw a copy of his first book of poems, Shaw found 'no sign that he had ever read anything later than Cowper or Crabbe, or even Byron, Shelley, or Keats ... There was indeed no sign of his ever having read anything otherwise than as a child reads.' But this was poetry. Who were Davies's mentors as far as prose was concerned? Who were his models? Shaw goes on to say that the autobiography is 'a placid narrative ... unvarnished in manner'. He says that 'it is only in verse' that Davies 'writes exquisitely' but that *The Autobiography* 'is worth reading for its style alone.' Nowhere, however, does Shaw attempt to examine this 'style' in any detail, and one suspects that few have.

Richard Stonesifer, however, has. In his *W.H. Davies: A Critical Biography* he devotes a whole chapter to the quality of Davies's prose, but although what he says is interesting and well worth reading, he concentrates on his manner rather than the actual content. It is certainly true that Davies tended to understate, to simplify, and to keep a distance from his reader. Nowhere does he give vent to passion or invective, and there is a kind of atmospheric objectivity about it all, as if it were happening to someone else. And this attitude, manner, or stance is something other than the actual vocabulary and syntax. It sets the tone, but the substance is something else.

Let's take Davies's description of a fight between him and Brum, both drunk, who were riding a train, and the car-man, who wanted to turn them off. The struggle takes place on the top of one of the carriages of a train which is moving at speed. Much the same scenario has played a part in many a Western, and we are all familiar with the dramatic situation.

'He was very near to us, when we sprang to our feet, and unexpectedly gripped him, one on each side, and before he could recover from his first astonishment. In all my life I have never seen so much fear on a human face. He must have seen our half-drunken condition and at once gave up all hopes of mercy from such men, for he stood helpless, not knowing what to do. If he struggled it would mean the fall and death of the three, and did he remain helpless in our hands, it might mean being thrown from that height from a car going at the rate of thirty miles an hour. "Now," said Brum, "what is it to be? Shall we ride this train without interference, or shall we have a wrestling bout up here, when the first fall must be our last? Speak?"'

The first thing to note is the extraordinarily calm manner in which this incident is narrated. This is achieved by Davies being explicit about the actual situation: the car-man was 'very near', he and Brum were 'one on each side', the train was 'going at the rate of thirty miles an hour' and Brum's alternatives are carefully stated. There is some energy in the description: they 'sprang' to their feet, they 'gripped' the man, who showed 'astonishment', but the adjectives are rather ordinary if we care to consider the truly terrifying circumstances. And Brum's alternatives could have been expressed in much more lively and colloquial language: 'Are you going to leave us be, or are we going to fight it out to the death?' Brum doesn't threaten the man. He doesn't say something like, 'I warn you' or 'Watch your step' or 'Keep away from us'. Instead he talks rather like a headmaster speaking to a recalcitrant pupil. There is a formality about it all which is inconsistent with the true situation.

Whatever other qualities Davies's prose might display, liveliness is not one of them. He appears to have written his narrative with great care, making sure of his punctuation, using a formal register, and making sure that he didn't give anything away. He is always a kind of detached observer. Notice how he describes himself and Brum as 'such men' in the description above. And, much later in his narrative, while he was staying at Rowton House, having settled there to write, Davies describes one of the residents as 'a very illiterate man, having no knowledge of grammar, punctuation, or spelling.' The description perhaps demonstrates his own attitude to the writing of prose: if you had a tale to tell, as he had, and you had a good knowledge of grammar, punctuation, and spelling, then you could be reasonably sure of success.

He really did have a tale to tell and, when the tale dictates the pace of the narrative and he forgets his customary preoccupation with what is careful and correct, Davies writes well. For instance he describes being dangerously ill with malaria with great economy and directness:

> ... I became too weak to move, and, coming to a large swamp, I left the railroad and crawled into it, and for three days and the same number of nights, lay there without energy to continue my journey. Wild hungry hogs were there, who approached dangerously near, but ran snorting away when my body moved. A score or more of buzzards had perched waiting on the branches above me, and I knew that the place was teeming with snakes. I suffered from a terrible thirst, and drank of the swamp pools, stagnant water that was full of germs, and had the colour of the rainbow, one dose of which would have poisoned some men to death.

Yet, once again, the writing is slightly spoiled by his being over-explicit. He lay there for exactly three days and three nights, there were twenty or more buzzards, the swamp pools were full of germs and then, interestingly, water 'which would have poisoned some men to death' but failed to kill the intrepid Davies. He was, after all, his own guarded hero.

In the 'Author's Note' Dawhich vies wrote for the 1920 edition of *The Autobiography*, he said that he had been

> ... very pleased to think that the book has not only been approved of by literary people, masters of schools and clergymen, but has also given pleasure to the more ordinary reader, including a great number of boys. The book has appealed to the former for a simple straightforward style, and to the latter for its spirit of adventure.

He also claims, in the same introduction, that when he wrote *The Autobiography* he 'had no more ambition in my prose at that time than I have now'.

This is, perhaps, somewhat ingenuous. Whilst it is true to say that Davies did regard himself as being predominantly a poet, he was nevertheless keen to achieve fame and earn money through whatever he wrote, regardless of whether it was prose or verse. It was simply that he first concentrated on poetry, believing that writing poems was the surest and easiest way to fame, but was persuaded by his literary friends that the story of his own adventurous life would substantially boost his literary presence as well as his income. He was nothing if not astute in these matters.

What is certain is that Davies never ever lost himself in his prose to the extent that he sometimes managed to do in his poetry, where he got closer to the emotional and psychological complexities of his nature. The characters he describes in *The Autobiography* are wooden creatures who, in spite of their strange (and possibly manufactured names) fail to come to life, although Davies is keen to describe their exploits. We finish *The Autobiography* knowing very little really, about Brum, the 'notorious beggar', New Haven Baldy who 'had a great reputation in the State of Connecticut', Australian Red 'a man above the average intelligence' and who 'seldom made an error in grammar or the pronunciation of words', Wee Scotty, Blackey, Cockney More who was 'a born thief', Philadelphia Slim, the Indian Kid, and so on. They are simply names to add substance to the adventures Davies describes. And of course, we learn very little about Davies himself, other than the chronology of events which make up his personal history.

The major event with which *The Autobiography* is concerned is the occasion when Davies lost a foot while attempting to jump a train, because this is what really changed his life forever.

After his companion, Three Fingered Jack, had jumped onto the train, Davies

> ... shouted to him to clear the step. This he proceeded to do, very deliberately, I thought. Taking a firmer grip on the bar, I jumped, but it was too late, for the train was now going at a rapid rate. My foot came short of the step, and I fell, and, still clinging to the handle bar, was dragged several yards before I relinquished my hold. And there I lay for several minutes, feeling a little shaken, while the train passed swiftly on into the darkness.

Notice that Three Fingered Jack 'proceeded to do' what Davies shouted about. Notice, also, that Davies didn't 'let go' but 'relinquished my hold'. And that, after this horrific experience, he felt 'a little shaken'! He 'attempted' not 'tried' to stand. He couldn't stand up because 'something had happened to prevent me from doing this' and when he discovered that 'the right foot was severed from the ankle' it 'did not shock me as much as the thoughts which quickly followed'. And when he is finally discovered and taken to the station waiting room while a doctor is contacted 'I could see no other way of keeping a calm face than by taking out my pipe and smoking'.

There is something extraordinarily complacent about all this in the circumstances, and the description very inadequately describes the situation. It is this lack of emotion in Davies's writing, as he contemplates this most dramatic of horrors, that arouses a curiosity in adult and sophisticated readers which is never truly satisfied. And that, perhaps, is one of the reasons why *The Autobiography* was so intriguing at the time, and became so for future generations. For 'the great number of boys' who, Davies said, enjoyed (and enjoy the book today), the book was, and is, the kind of uncluttered tale that appeals. As, of course, it does to girls. Both like stories which are purely narrative, without much description and, preferably, no depth of characterisation. Boys, especially, like plain facts, which is what Davies gives them. They enjoy action and they like 'characters' who 'do' things. And the kind of 'character' Davies, the narrator, presents them with, allows them to engage with the narrative: they become, in fantasy, Davies himself. And it is they who imaginatively adopt Davies's 'coolness' in the midst of danger and adversity. For Davies never allows himself to be seen as genuinely weak or truly vulnerable. He always, through courage and determination, survives. He is proud, in the way that young boys would like to be proud.

As for the actual style of the writing – well, very few young readers are particularly interested in nuances of style. It doesn't bother them too much if the style of a book seems outdated or quaint, as long as the story line is strong enough. And Davies's style is, sometimes, quite odd. Take this paragraph, for instance:

> We now entered the 'Cock', and after calling for two glasses of ale, enquired as to accommodation for travellers, which we were informed was good, there being plenty of room. Sometimes, if ale is not called for, they are disinclined to letting beds, especially in the winter, when they find so little difficulty in filling the house.

This is a clumsy piece of writing. There is nothing of the grace and fluidity one would expect from a more sophisticated writer, and Davies is unable to adopt the informal colloquial style which would be more appropriate for the occasion. They didn't 'go into' the pub and 'ask for' two pints. They didn't 'ask about rooms'. They were told that the 'accommodation for travellers ... was good'. And notice Davies's fondness for '-ing' form constructions: 'after calling', 'there being', 'disinclined to letting' and 'difficulty in filling'. Such constructions are a peculiarity of his rather formal and stilted style.

No, Davies was no stylist. Doggedly, throughout this book, he progresses from incident to incident with the same inflexibility, describing events and circumstances in his curious, idiosyncratic way. A useful comparison might be with the prose of Thomas Hardy, much maligned for his, sometimes, syntactical incongruities and odd vocabulary. But no-one today doubts the value of his prose. Its power is derived from the tortured emotions which drive it.

With Davies's prose, it is different. What attracts readers and gives this book its enduring life is the very opposite of what ensures the permanence of Hardy's prose: it is the entrancingly understated originality of a true-life narrative which clothes the actual horrors of its content with prose which is of the plainest kind. If you want to find out what happened to Davies, during his childhood and adolescence in Newport, aboard cattle boats, tramping from place to place both in the USA and England and Wales, then *The Autobiography* will give you something of the truth. If you want to know what it was like to be an unpublished writer, struggling to achieve some kind of recognition then, again, *The Autobiography* will give you the facts. Whether the 'facts' are actually true is another matter; the point is that they 'feel' true. In other words, *The Autobiography* has its own idiosyncratic identity. There is, simply, nothing quite like it.

There were other prose books, though. *Beggars* was published by Duckworth in 1909, and *The True Traveller* in 1912. Of these two books, Davies wrote (in the Foreword to a third book, *The Adventures of Johnny Walker, Tramp* (hereafter called *Johnny Walker* and published by Cape in 1926)

> ... when I come to mention the other two books, *Beggars* and *The True Traveller*, it is a different matter ... there was one strong point against them – the essay form was used more than the narrative, and people preferred the latter. In doing this book ... I have used the experiences selected in *Beggars* and *The True Traveller*, but I have destroyed the essay form and made the book run as a story.

5

Johnny Walker and Other Tales

A Poet's Pilgrimage (1918) describes a walking journey Davies took in Wales and, in the later part of the book, back in England. He started from London and took the train to Carmarthen. From Carmarthen, he walked to Llanelli, Swansea, Neath, Aberdare, Merthyr, Tredegar, Ebbw Vale, Abergavenny, Monmouth, Tintern, Chepstow, and finally ended up in his home-town of Newport. From Newport, he travelled east towards England, via Pontypool and Cardiff, from where he took the train to Bristol to begin the walk back to London. At Maidenhead, he decided to finish walking and took the train for the final part of the journey.

In a way, it's the same old Davies we have become used to. In terms of content, there are modern equivalents: commissioned books based on recorded experiences in particular circumstances. These days, a publisher might commission a book about sleeping rough for a year, or working as a hospital porter, or travelling through Europe on a canal boat. Television programmes are based on similar experiences. In *A Poet's Pilgrimage* Davies tries to repeat the kind of tramping life he wrote about in *The Autobiography* but, this time, he stays in rented accommodation rather than common lodging houses, and the people he meets and consorts with are simply folk he meets on the way.

His eye for natural beauty was extraordinarily conventional and his descriptions of the countryside were very much like those found in coffee-table guide books of the time. For example:

> When I reached the *Clytha Arms*, which was a superior-looking and beautiful hotel, and nothing like the usual wayside inn, I could not help being struck by the beauty all around me. I saw the river Usk in a valley, with cattle and sheep in the fields on either side, and some of the sheep were walking on the clean, silvery stones at the riverside. Sometimes I saw old leafy walls, the boundaries of large estates, and I was often shaded by chestnut blossoms instead of common leaves. In fact, I sometimes thought I was not on the King's Highway at all, but trespassing in a nobleman's park.

Notice that the hotel was 'superior looking', that the riverside stones were 'clean', that the chestnut blossoms were not 'common leaves' and that he felt as if he was in 'a nobleman's park'. Later on, he comes across an old accordion player who is playing for money. Davies, patronising as usual, had already given the man a penny for his pains, and says to the man, '"You play that instrument very well," which was a lie'. The accordion player says that he would play even better if he was well-dressed and paid in gold, but he plays to suit the circumstances. Davies encourages the man to play at his best. When he does, Davies says the playing is '"Very good", although I had heard scores of uneducated farm labourers and costermongers play better'. Davies 'knew that no audience, however rough and uneducated, would have listened to such music for more than five minutes ... ' But he eggs the man on, and we are treated to more than a page or two of Davies's mockery, even to the extent of his giving the accordion player another penny before sending him on his way. The ridiculous conceit of the accordion player is, somehow, capped by the patronising conceit of Davies himself.

But Davies can tell a tale. For example, at Tintern, he meets up with a man who is fond of fishing. The man is standing on a bridge, looking down into the river Monnow. This man tells Davies an extraordinary story about a very large trout, which Davies retells with relish. No-one was able to catch this trout for three days. '"But on the third day a friend of mine, who was the fattest man in Monmouth and weighed forty-seven stone ... in less than half an hour (caught) that trout, which weighed five pounds ... "' How did he do it? '"My friend's bait was a long tapeworm taken out of a live sheep."'

This is typical Davies. Earlier he met a little boy who asked him what was wrong with his leg. Davies explains that '"an engine ran over it"' and the little boy replies '"Suppose it had been your head?"' Davies, tellingly, makes no comment and leaves reflection, amused or otherwise, to the reader. And when his fishing acquaintance tells a similar story about the same fat man catching an enormous salmon in the river Wye, Davies comes 'to the conclusion that the river Wye had inspired fishermen as well as poets'.

Those who are tempted to make much of Davies's Welshness might be somewhat put off by what he says about Ty-yn-y-Pwll

Inn. To him

> ... it is as surely Welsh as Patrick Flanagan is Irish. I tried
> to pronounce it, but had to give it up in despair, coming
> to the conclusion that as there is no accounting for the
> way such names are pronounced, I should be quite likely
> to be near the mark if I called it Jones or Smith.

Tell *that* to a true, Welsh-speaking Welshman! But, of course,
Davies spoke no Welsh and was always happier in the company
of English speakers.

Always ready for a tale – even if it was a tall one – Davies tells
the story of Gutto Nyth Bran, 'the famous runner', who won a
race from Newport bridge to Bedwas Bridge against 'the champion
of all England'. He wins but, when 'one old dame' congratulates
him by clapping him on the back, Gutto collapses 'and when
they picked him up he was dead'. A little later, he tells us that
most of 'the poorer classes' in Wales normally wear black 'because
they pay so much respect to the dead in attending funerals that
every man is expected to have a suit of black in readiness at a
moment's notice'. Maybe.

A Poet's Pilgrimage is hardly more than a fairly average kind
of travel book, unusual only in the sense that the man writing it
had once been a tramp and had decided to do most of the journey
on foot. Unusual, too, in that it was written by an ex-tramp who
had become something of a literary celebrity. Yet the style of the
book has little to recommend it. It lacks the fluency of *Johnny
Walker*, written about eight years later, and the writing is
reminiscent, sometimes, of the clumsy manner common in *The
Autobiography*.

The cumulative effect of Davies's rather leisurely, old-fashioned, and quaintly conservative style of writing does give this book the kind of oddity which many readers might find attractive. Surprisingly, much of it is included in *The Essential W.H. Davies*, published by Cape in 1951, but nothing at all from *Johnny Walker*, a better written and more professional piece of work.

Later Days is the title of a book published by Jonathan Cape in 1925. Three years prior to this, Cape had become Davies's publisher, and remained so until some years after his death. They published *The Hour of Magic*, a book of poems, in 1922, followed by *True Travellers: A Tramps Opera*, in 1923. In the same year, Cape published the *Collected Poems* in two volumes. Davies was becoming a serious commercial proposition.

Later Days contains much interesting and significant biographical detail, including interesting portraits of Davies's literary contemporaries. It is as anecdotal as *Johnny Walker*, and written in a similar style. Davies came to write his prose much as he talked, and one can imagine him, glass of beer in one hand and pipe in the other, telling these stories to an inquisitive listener at one of the many literary gatherings he was invited to. Similar ground to that covered in *Johnny Walker*, published a year after *Later Days*, had already been covered in *A Poet's Pilgrimage*, published in 1918, and *Later Days* completes what might be regarded as a trilogy. All are worth reading, but *Later Days* is the most significant in that it records a period of literary history from the point of view of a writer who fully shared in it.

Davies's editors at Jonathan Cape were responsible for *Later Days* and the effect of good professional advice and careful editing shows. Apart from the interesting literary material in the book, which makes it something of a must for literary historians and biographers, there is a certain lightness and confidence about it which is attractive, after the heavy style of his previous prose work. Those clumsy idiosyncracies which mar the earlier work, in spite of their quaintness, are still there but they have been either toned down or edited out. Davies, one feels, is genuinely enjoying himself in this book while, at the same time, indulging his (and our) appetite for gossip and malice. To his natural arrogance and pride, he adds a stinging wit and a capacity for revealing hypocrisy and insincerity.

In 'Works of Art' and 'Artists All' we are taken on a sort of light-hearted tour of names and anecdotes, without much serious penetration. Davies appears to appreciate the work of artists like Sickert, but the appreciation is as much to do with Sickert's reputation as with his painting. Davies likes his readers to know that he has had more than a nodding acquaintance with influential artists. And in spite of his insistence that he was not a name-dropper, he certainly was. He much enjoyed the company of the aristocracy: Lady Richie, Lord Crewe, Lady Cunard, Lord Balfour, Sir Robert Horne, and the like. However, we learn little about these people – artists or otherwise – other than that they are characters in yet another of Davies's collection of amusing anecdotes.

Although we can never be sure that Davies, when appearing serious, is not writing with his tongue in his cheek, we can usually be certain that his stories will be well worth the telling. Some of them are more than memorable. Particularly amusing is the tale of Nobby George, who was one of Davies's shipmates on his Atlantic crossings. Nobby George was a renowned fighter and

Davies's companions, or anyone else for that matter, would think twice before mixing things with Nobby. 'Why does the sporting man,' Davies asks, make so much of boxers who are tall, well-built, and generally physically impressive? Few of them would have beaten Nobby George. And why? Because Nobby was not only left-handed, but cross-eyed as well.

> Where is the scientific fighter who can stand up before a left-handed man who is also cross-eyed? If you cannot catch his eye, how can you forestall his movements. Every side-step we make, to catch his eye, is only wasted breath. He appears to be looking elsewhere, and yet we know he is closely watching us all the time.

The last two chapters of *Later Days* are taken up with Davies's description of a severe illness he suffered from while living in his rented accommodation in London, the subsequent near death of his young housekeeper, the unpleasant nature of her replacement, and the news that he had decided to get married to a much younger woman and was leaving London for a village in Sussex. The book ends with a somewhat sentimental evocation of their idyllic life in the English countryside. But, as usual with Davies, and much as we would expect, the truth was something different and only to be found in a book which was not published until 1980, forty years after the author's death. That book was *Young Emma*, possibly the most interesting and the closest to the truth of all Davies's prose work. But more of that later.

The blurb on the cover of *The Adventures of Johnny Walker, Tramp* (1926) states that its predecessor, *The Autobiography of a Super Tramp*, 'has never had any sensational sale. It has, however, gone on selling steadily a few hundred copies each year for nearly twenty years. Today (1926) its yearly sale is larger than at any time before'. The blurb says that '*Johnny Walker* should be read straight off as a story of adventure. It is the realisation of true experiences, and all its characters have or have had a real existence'.

But can it really 'be read straight off as a story of adventure'? It appears to consist, after all, of a series of topics arranged as chapters. The first chapter begins in Chicago, but the second begins to drift and, by the third, we come to assume that the book will draw on various experiences Davies had during his tramping days, without the chronological, narrative format of *The Autobiography*. In a way, this covers different ground from *The Autobiography* and, no doubt, that was what Davies was trying to do. But he might have felt that the book would become nothing more than random tramping stories selected from memory – or even fabricated. He needed to have some kind of thematic structure to hold the thing together. Hence the attempt first of all to make comparisons between tramping in England and America, then to extend this into a treatment of different general themes. But, somehow, this isn't successful, and the book becomes little more than additions to the tramping stories he told in *The Autobiography*. No doubt this happened because he was transforming the essays which made up *Beggars* (1909) and *The True Traveller* (1912), those earlier books which were far less successful than *The Autobiography*.

What is missing, however, is the absolute conviction that we are reading a first-hand account of a man's actual life. This is not to suggest that *Johnny Walker* is fictitious. Of course not. But one has to remember that there was no-one to verify whether

Davies was always telling the truth or not and, knowing Davies (as we do from the recollections of friends and others) we are well aware that he was not above embellishing things somewhat. After all, he knew that what made him interesting and different was the fact that he had actually been a tramp, begged, lodged in common lodging houses and so on for years. None of his contemporaries who were writers had had anything like his extraordinary experiences and adventures. And he had, in addition, lost a leg in the process and had the evidence to prove it. He was, almost without saying, 'a character'.

The style is vigorous enough to tempt any alert reader to follow the story further. Davies had learnt the art of leading us on by encouraging and then satisfying (after enough delay to whet our appetites) our curiosity and Davies is not above telling what one might call 'a tall story', like the one about a man 'so dirty and ragged that he was a disgrace to third-rate begggars' and who had 'long matted hair and beard'. This man 'suddenly became ambitious for fame' and was determined not only to sleep in a clean, comfortable bed, but 'to wake the next morning famous like Byron' (shades of Davies himself?). He got into the grounds of a rich man's estate, managed to find his way into the house, and finally slept in one of the beds all night before being disturbed in the morning by one of the servants. Stories like this one (taken from the chapter: 'Strokes of Genius') occur throughout *Johnny Walker* but readers had to wait for more than fifty years before a book was published which has the kind of integrity and honesty of Davies's best poems.

6

Young Emma

Young Emma, probably the most significant of Davies's prose works, was not published until 1980. The postscript to the book reads: 'This is the end of my story, told bluntly and honestly, and without exaggeration. For I have always been honest and sincere in my literary work, without thinking of popularity ... ' But although the first sentence is certainly true, the second is more than doubtful. *Young Emma* is important not only because of its fascinating content but also because it reveals much of the real Davies behind the mask. Davies was a very shy man and very protective of his public image. He was also a survivor and knew how to make the most of whatever chances were given to him, in literature as well as on the road. So the apparently suicidal act of wanting to publish *Young Emma* is surprising. Why would he want to do that? Why was Davies keen for the public to know that he had suffered from venereal disease, that he had been in the fairly regular habit of sleeping with prostitutes, and that he had, finally, married a prostitute who was twenty-eight years younger than he was.

There is no doubt that his publisher, Jonathan Cape, was shocked by the manuscript. He feared for Davies's reputation if the book was published and decided to see what George Bernard Shaw (who had so successfully promoted *The Autobiography*) thought about it. Shaw, who was canny in these matters and professionally astute, advised against it. In the meantime, Davies told his wife what was happening, and her extreme anxiety made Davies nervous. Terrified that the story might get into the wrong hands, he asked Jonathan Cape to destroy it. Cape returned the original but kept two copies of the manuscript which, having been kept in a safe, resurfaced eighteen years later when Cape handed it to C.V.Wedgewood, who was on the staff.

Wedgewood much admired it but thought that publication while Davies's wife was still alive was out of the question. Davies had died two years before, but his wife was still middle-aged and likely to live for some time. She didn't, in fact, die until 1979. There is no doubt that without this book our assessment of Davies would be fundamentally incomplete.

The story begins during the First World War when, according to Davies, prostitutes preferred the company of soldiers rather than civilians. In any case, Davies was middle-aged, short and stocky, and had a wooden leg: hardly attractive attributes. But, as was his custom, he was often out and about very late at night, looking for a bed-mate. It isn't surprising that Davies found himself, in such circumstances, mixed up with odd characters, and he describes his encounters directly and honestly.

However, although Davies told the truth in this book, he told it in such a way that he kept hidden the darker implications of what he described. He always did that. He says that 'I always like to spend my money as though I am worth plenty more', which is disarmingly honest but hardly damning. Again, 'I cannot hold my water long enough for a prolonged conversation' is a statement which arouses our amused concern, but tells us little. And again: 'Now, although I am a rough man in some ways, that can boast of neither college nor club, yet, for all that, I have been called more than once "one of Nature's gentlemen". Which means, I suppose, that I am a gentle man.'

Behind all these 'charming' sentiments lives a man who is more than a casual drinker, who spends a lot of his time cruising the streets late at night looking for a prostitute, and who married a young, innocent girl who was nearly thirty years his junior. Yet he is intent on making it clear, when he begins the story of his encounter with his future wife, that he wasn't 'the strong, crafty, designing man of middle age on the look-out for a young and innocent girl'. One takes it all with the proverbial pinch of salt.

Anyway, when he does meet the woman he calls 'Emma' ('Dinah' in the poems and 'Helen' in real life) he calculates that she 'could be anything between fifteen and twenty years of age'. He meets her while he is on his customary search for a prostitute, but not one who was the worse for drink. Whether he was truly on the lookout for a future wife, as he assures us in this book that he was, is by no means certain. What is certain is that Helen's attitude towards him gradually encouraged him to feel that their relationship could be permanent. As, indeed, it was.

When he asks Helen where she is going, and she tells him that she has spent the evening with friends and is on her way home, he says: 'Will you come to my home instead?' Her simple, apparently trustful, reply, and the way she immediately takes his arm, impresses Davies. And it is this that changes his attitude towards her, whatever his intentions had been (and one can imagine what they were). Not that he was comfortable about it all: 'I began to wonder what people thought of seeing a well-dressed man of middle age walking side by side with a young girl that was poorly dressed.' He goes on to say that Helen was, in fact, twenty-three, although he could not have known that at the time.

Davies was a very shy man, especially with women. He was comfortable with prostitutes because they made no emotional demands on him, and he was free to pick one of them up whenever he felt the sexual need. Their relationship was simply a business one. That was how he wanted it, although he always appears to have treated them with respect and, more than once, speaks of their kindness to him. With Helen, it became more than that because of her character, the fact that she was young and beautiful, and because of her absolute loyalty to him. Her simplicity and genuine affection for him created within him the possibility of getting away from London into 'the green country' and living a simple life with a woman who was prepared to look after him and see to his needs. He needed someone he could depend on and, in return, was prepared to provide for her. His intentions weren't all that different from those he had previously harboured, when his female companions were little more than housekeepers and sexual servants, but Helen encouraged him to aspire to something more than that. He could, at last, become the kind of established country poet he had dreamed of becoming, far away from the noisy, crowded streets of London and his unsatisfactory little flat above a shop. He could become a sort of Horace and live in bucolic happiness. But things were not quite as straightforward as he had hoped they would be. The horrors of venereal disease interrupted his aspirations and threatened the relationship between the middle-aged poet and his young mistress.

The fact that Helen didn't drink and was unsophisticated and undemanding impressed Davies. He was convinced that she was not a 'professional street walker' because if she had been 'her mouth would have been firm and hard, and no softer for a smile that was forced and false'. She was also in work, but dissatisfied with her wages. Davies was certain that her low wages must be the reason why she slept with men from time to time. When Davies discovered that she intended giving in her notice, he suggested that she come and live with him, telling her that if she was prepared to 'look after my comfort, you will be certain to find a kind and an easy master'.

Helen agrees to come and live with Davies in a week's time and, in her absence, he finds it difficult to be patient. He finds his good fortune in finding Helen difficult to believe and suspects that he has, once again, been tricked. His fears are further strengthened by discovering that he has venereal disease. Convinced that Helen is responsible, his expectations of her returning are poor and he curses himself for being hoodwinked. How could a man with his experience of life be tricked by a young girl?

But she does return, looking as innocent as ever. He is overjoyed to see her but when he confronts her with the facts of his disease, partly in concern for her, she is quite unperturbed. Why would she have come back to him if she had been responsible?

The relationship between Davies and Helen develops into a strong and affectionate partnership but Davies's health complicates matters. One of the effects of venereal disease has been a poisoned and swollen foot, which causes him considerable pain. Walking becomes impossible and he becomes totally reliant on Helen. He loses the use of his arms, but her patient and loving nursing strengthens further the strong bond between them. And then Helen herself becomes very ill.

She is in great pain. She is unable to look after Davies any longer and he, in desperation, gets his own doctor in to see what can be done. The doctor treats her but warns that if she isn't taken to hospital immediately she will bleed to death. The manageress of the shop downstairs, who has been giving her whatever help she can, tries to get Helen admitted to one of the London hospitals. They are full. Then the police are contacted and, after a series of practical complications, Helen is taken away by ambulance.

It is at this stage of the story that the shop manageress informs Davies that Helen was pregnant. The doctor removed the foetus and consequently Helen haemorrhaged. All this sets Davies thinking: so that was why Helen wanted to leave her job, and that was why she had relied on Davies's kindness to save her from an impossible situation. What will happen when Helen is well again and no longer needs to be dependent on him?

While Helen is in hospital, Davies engages another housekeeper who is happy to have the work. It is in her own interests that he remains disabled for as long as possible. She is a diligent and efficient servant, but he becomes increasingly worried about her future. What will happen when Helen returns?

When his doctor comes to visit him, Davies tells him that Helen is the cause of his illness. The doctor informs him that, if that is the case, her expectation of life might well be something like seven years. Davies asks the doctor to make the hospital aware of the situation, so that she can be treated before it's too late. He does so, but Davies hears nothing futher. He has had a letter from Helen, however, and he has sent her some money.

Two more letters follow and, eventually, Helen returns to the flat. Davies, to the consternation of his housekeeper, is overjoyed. But he is also very concerned, although he doesn't, at first, share his concerns with Helen. What he does tell her is that a friend (it was Edward Thomas) has found a house for Davies in the country. Will she go with him?

When she immediately agrees, Davies feels free to pursue the question of her pregnancy. It turns out that the father wanted to marry her but she refused him. Davies has had enough experience of the seamier side of life not to be too censorious about this kind of thing, and is satisfied with her directness and honesty. The man in question had been the son of a woman Helen knew through her daughter. One day, when she had decided to visit, the mother and daughter were out, but the son was in, and he took advantage of her in their absence. Davies's comment is interesting:

> If an ordinary man, in civilian's clothes, had used her too
> freely with his hands, she probably would have smacked
> his face and called him a dirty beast. But with a young
> officer, who had served his country and been employed
> in destroying her enemies, the case was different.

Life in the country for the two of them was much as both of them expected, but there were still shadows over their future. Davies was still something of an invalid and when he developed further symptoms which suggested his venereal disease had returned, he mentioned the matter to Helen, suggesting that she herself should seek medical attention. They had intended to get married, but Davies decided to delay this until they had both been given a clean bill of health.

Helen, in fact, was totally innocent. She had never had venereal disease. And Davies's new symptoms happened to be benign, too. But until matters cleared up, their relationship became turbulent and they were both sulky and quarrelsome. Davies harboured suspicions that tormented him and Helen was disturbed by Davies's attitude.

The story has a happy ending, however, and like all good stories they get married and live happily ever after. Well, it's not quite as simple as that, but each of them found in the other that complementarity which is the basis of all good marriages. But Davies, possibly, sacrificed more than Helen did. The business of looking after Davies and being a good houswife, in return for financial and emotional security, appears to have cost her little. Davies, on the other hand, has to behave himself and, in return for the domestic comforts which Helen gave him, he had to forgo his drinking habits, his forays into London society (and low life) and to live the life of a respectable married man.

7

Davies the Georgian

Country retirement, in combination with his established reputation as a literary figure, had a damaging effect on Davies's poems. He regularly turned them out, but their quality became dependent on their marketability and the popular poetic conventions of the time. He had to remain the Davies that his publishers had made fashionable. But fashions were changing and, during the Thirties, Davies had already become a much-anthologised remnant of a literary generation that had seen its popularity dramatically decline. He was, as were those others (with very few exceptions) who had been published in Edward Marsh's *Georgian* anthologies, an ageing remnant of a now dishonoured tribe.

But, strangely, *Young Emma*, might have made a difference. It is an attractive, and often moving, story and it demonstrates what is best in Davies as a writer: his rugged individualism, what has been described as his 'peasant shrewdness', his unblinking courage in the face of bitter experience, his authentic experience of poverty and degradation, his sheer doggedness in the face of adversity and, above all, his odd way of looking at things which distinguishes his poetry from those of his contemporaries. For Davies, in spite of all that can be said against him, was the real thing. The problem is to distinguish the true metal from the dross.

Davies was published in all five of Edward Marsh's collections of what he called *Georgian Poetry*, and he was given generous space. The five separate volumes were published between 1911 and 1922, and the kinds of poems included in those anthologies have come to be regarded as generic of a much-maligned strain in English verse. The strain might be said to continue to this day, wherever amateur poets gather to read together and distribute verse which fails to attract commercial publishers. Such verse, apart from often being technically flawed, is intellectually unchallenging, commonplace in its observations of life, and sentimental. Yet it is surprising how few are the discerning readers who can discriminate between verse of this kind and what might be called 'poetry'. As long ago as 1929, I.A. Richards in *Practical Criticism* demonstrated that Cambridge undergraduates were as likely to misinterpret and misjudge poems as anyone else. And, in spite of something like a century of 'academic criticism' and generations of sixth form and university students trained to read and judge poems, evaluation of the work of modern poets is as subject to moods and fashions as it was in the days of Edward Marsh. There is a currency built around the tastes of poetry editors, poets and reviewers (who are, as often as not, the same people) which validates and promotes, irrespective of minority counter claims and individual dissent. Edward Marsh has his own taste in poetry, and the five issues of *Georgian Poetry* simply illustrate one man's ideas of what poetry should be like. What has come to be known as 'Georgian Poetry' has been defined by those poets of the 1920s and 1930s who rebelled against it, rather than by those poets who were chosen for the Marsh anthologies. One would look in vain in any of Davies's prose writings for a working definition of 'poetry'. He knew what he liked, and he imitated those poets he was instinctively attracted to (as with most poets) but he was also a victim of the tastes of those who chose to publish his poems. Since he earned his living principally by writing and publishing poems, he was naturally reluctant to write poems which he knew would offend the taste of his publishers. He was a victim of fashion, just as much as any other poet is.

To read through the poems of his which Marsh chose for *Georgian Poetry* (and Davies was one of the major contributors to all five volumes) is to recognise the Davies of future anthologies, as well as the Davies who contributed to practically every literary magazine of his time. His fame declined throughout the 1930s, as 'Modernism' itself became a fashion, and as the poetry scene became dominated by politically committed poets. The poets who survived, either because they were favoured by academic critics or because they had qualities which were seen to be less at variance with current fashion, managed to shed their associations with the 'Georgians' in spite of their close friendships with, and admiration for, poets who had been popularised by Marsh. Edward Thomas, perhaps, is an exception in that, although he knew most of Marsh's favourites personally, and promoted their work, he was never published by Marsh. Whether that stood in his favour with later poets and critics is another matter.

It is helpful, when we are trying to test the worth of Davies as

a poet, to always bear in mind that he was regarded by Thomas
as one of the better poets of the time and, although Thomas
respected talents which are tarnished by today's standards (he
was one of the judges who awarded a *Poetry Review* prize to
Rupert Brooke's 'Grantchester') he also wrote favourable reviews
of modernist poets like Ezra Pound. Thomas was uncommonly
familiar with the whole of English literature, as well as knowing
much of French and German literature as well, and his
appreciation of the poems of Robert Frost, whose poetry had
hitherto been ignored by the American literary establishment,
shows unusual discrimination. And Thomas knew *why* he thought
Frost was special, and was able to effectively explain his advocacy
in print. The reasons why Thomas thought so much of Davies
need to be carefully examined if we are to evaluate Davies's true
worth.

Certainly Thomas was attracted by Davies's circumstances and
his colourful past, and he was something of a nomadic romantic
himself, liking nothing better than to roam the countryside in
solitude. Constricted as he was by family responsibilities and the
arduous necessity of earning enough to support his wife and
family, the apparently free-spirited Davies, with his gypsy-like
appearance and seemingly rustic forthrightness, must have
appealed to Thomas's restless sensibility.

When Davies's second book, *New Poems*, was published in
1907, Thomas recommended the following poems to his friend,
W.H. Hudson: 'The Ways of Time', 'Ale', 'The Likeness', 'The
Ox', 'The Calm', 'Violet to the Bee', 'Music', 'New-comers',
'Parted', and 'Catharine'. (All these poems may be found within
pages 53 and 64 of the *Complete Poems* published by Cape in

1963, except for 'The Calm' which appears on page 582 and 'Violet to the Bee' which appears on page 588.)

This is a suprising choice. Reviewing Davies's first collection (*The Soul's Destroyer*, 1905) for the *Daily Chronicle*, Thomas said:

> He has travelled: he knows Wales, London, America, and Hell. These things and many more his poems tell us; and to see him is to see a man from whom unskilled labour in America, work in Atlantic cattle boats, and a dire London life, have not taken away the earnestness, the tenderness, or the accent of a typical Monmouthshire man. His greatness rests upon a wide humanity, a fresh and unbiassed observation, and a noble use of the English tongue. His humanity is so wide that, though he writes much about himself, he is less egoistic than another man who writes of fair Rosamond or Medea. He can write commonplace and inaccurate English; but it is also natural to him to write, much as Wordsworth wrote, with the clearness, compactness, and facility which make a man think with shame how unworthily, through natural stupidity or uncertainty, he manages his native tongue. In subtlety he abounds.

This is high praise indeed. But, although there is some truth in what Thomas says, it is reasonable to doubt some of its excesses. Yes, Davies had travelled and his poems (the best of them, perhaps) do tell us something of this, and he had certainly experienced more than his share of Hell (again, present in the better poems), but he was never a willing labourer and always did his best to shirk that kind of work. Nor should one make too much of his Welshness: he may have had an Monmouthsire accent but he never expressed any desire to make his home in Wales. Again, Davies hardly wrote 'inaccurate' English, although he wasn't above writing a stilted kind of prose sometimes. He prided himself on writing grammatical English, and that pride was surely justified. As for Wordsworth, well, Davies doesn't appear to have been drawn to his work, preferring Elizabethan lyrics, Shakespeare's songs, and especially the poetry of Herrick: he liked his poetry to be musical rather than philosophical. T.S. Eliot said of the Georgians that 'The Georgian Love of Nature is on the whole less vague than Wordworth's, and has less philosphy behind it', and that is surely true.

One of the poems Thomas recommended to Hudson was 'The Likeness'. It's a short poem of only three stanzas, and is worth quoting in full for the sake of comparison with what I believe are far stronger poems in *New Poems* (which, incidentally, is dedicated to Helen and Edward Thomas). Here it is:

> When I came forth this morn I saw
> Quite twenty cloudlets in the air;
> And then I saw a flock of sheep,
> Which told me how those clouds came there.
>
> That flock of sheep, on that green grass,
> Well it might lie so still and proud!
> Its likeness had been drawn in heaven,
> On a blue sky, in silvery cloud.
>
> I gazed me up, I gazed me down,
> And swore, though good the likeness was,
> 'Twas a long way from justice done
> To such white wool, such sparkling grass.

The first things to notice about this poem are the archaisms: 'came forth', 'this morn', the strange 'I gazed me up, I gazed me down', and the contraction ''Twas'. The poem, like so many of Davies's lyrics, has the flavour of the Elizabethan about it. But the idea (or 'conceit') is typically Davies's own: that the sheep in the green meadow are like white clouds descended from the blue sky. Such odd, and essentially poetic, conjuctions are common in Davies : 'butterflies are but winged flowers', the robin's breast is 'like one red apple' as he perches in the leafless apple tree, and the 'cruel rose bud' has a 'close hard heart'. They reveal a way of seeing which is a major element in Davies's originality and they are what has made so many of his poems attractive as anthology pieces. But, at their best, these metaphorical concentrations have a Shakespearian power and they remind one of the best in Blake's *Songs of Innocence and Experience*. It is that 'compactness' which Thomas speaks of and gives Davies his ability to bring together diverse elements of perception into a kind of imaginative fusion. In his ability to do this, Davies is extraordinary in the best sense, and it is a certain mark of his importance.

Yet, in this poem which Thomas has quite deliberately chosen, the thought is commonplace and there is nothing of that imaginative power which we look for in the best of Davies's poems. It is pretty, but without mystery or originality, and it is the kind of poem which has disguised Davies's true worth. There is a triteness about it which depletes its poetic worth.

Of the poems from this volume which Thomas chose to highlight, only three have that mark of authenticity by which Davies's best work must be judged. The poems Thomas chose are, in the main, typical Davies nature-pieces. They contain the relatively few but constantly recurring elements from Nature which Davies continuously reused in poem after poem throughout his writing career: birds in general, flowers in general, butterflies, Nature with a capital 'N', robins, apples and apple blossom, primroses, anemones, violets, bees, poppies, nightingales, swallows and, of course, sheep and lambs. One could easily compile a complete inventory of these items from the natural scene. And again, Thomas has chosen poems which, when they are not sentimental, come very close to being so, with themes like the nostalgia for childhood, breeding cattle for meat, the death of a little girl, the simplicity and peace of Nature contrasted with the noise and violence of the city, the sadness of the passage of the seasons, and so on. These are subjects which Davies returned to again and again. They are the stuff of poetry, but not its life. The life, in Davies, was somewhere else, and the titles of some of the poems which Thomas chose not to mention give us a clue: 'The Forsaken Dead', 'The Dying', 'The Homeless Man', 'Saturday Night in the Slums', 'Whiskey', 'Hope Abandoned'. In similar poems, Davies is not escaping to 'Nature' but recalling the 'Hell' which Thomas mentions. Here 'green mosses ooze and spread/ Out of the pores of their decaying walls', the dying man 'fumbles in the clothes for want of thought', the homeless man is 'worn to a rag and bone' and, in the slums old age 'has a blackened eye/ And that grey hair is stained with gore'.

Thomas, though, did choose 'Ale' as one of his favourites, and this has the kind of energy that too few of Davies's poems have. When it is there, we are grateful for it. This is a robust, 'devil may care' Davies, with money in his pocket and the freedom to spend it:

> Life is a shade; Death wears the flesh;
> But a quart of ale puts flesh on me,
> And gives me power then to outgrin
> That ugly grinner Death, when he
> Doth as some passing shadow seem,
> Whereas 'tis *Life* is a thin dream.

'Music', too, ends magnificently as, after a somewhat commonplace preamble, Davies suddenly rises to the occasion:

> Life's river, with its early rush,
> Falls into a mysterious hush
> When nearing the eternal sea:
> Yet we would not forgetful be,
> In these deep, silent days so wise,
> Of shallows making mighty noise
> When we were young, when we were gay,
> And never thought Death lived – that day.

Wordsworth himself, perhaps, would not have been ashamed of those lines. They are evidence, if evidence were needed, that Davies at his best is a poet of genuine power. He is able to sustain the emotion through a sweep of eight melodic lines until the beautifully modulated, and affecting, conclusion: the sadness is convincing, and the poem has a fine integrity.

The gift of being more than a Georgian bucolic country lover leaning on a gate to survey the rural scene is Davies's privilege, had those who made so much of him been prepared to see it. He did, of course, like to escape to the country, but it was perhaps that eventual perpetual retreat into its green and quiet security which killed him as a poet. He had been a man who had mixed with the roughest and meanest, and he had the scars to prove it –

scars which are the mark of that other Davies, who viewed
mankind with a mixture of scepticism, wit, and not a little
humour, as in another poem ('Scotty Bill' which Thomas missed):

> There's 'Scotty' Bill, four score of years,
> Who, every morn that we arise,
> Will swear that summer's not yet come,
> And questions us – 'Where are the flies?'

– for 'Scotty' Bill makes his living by selling sticky fly-papers!
This is a Bill who 'knows a thing or two' and Davies would 'back
Bill for a hundred years' if he had 'better food and half a home'.
Davies skilfully controls the story throughout this short poem of
six stanzas, and the reader is captivated. We are in the presence
of the true Davies: the man who liked nothing better than, pint
of ale in hand, to recount his memories of the odd characters and
events he had experienced in an unusually eventful early life. It's
a tall story maybe, but a lively one. And Davies, once he got going,
was a lively character. But he was principally a town-dweller,
brought up by an eccentric sea-going grandfather, and the pulse
of urban life as well as life aboard ship did more for his spirits
than any amount of listening to nightingales. He loved the country,
but principally as a place to reflect on his past adventures, but his
public wanted something different and he had talent enough to
supply them with what they wanted. They wanted a Georgian,
and he was prepared to pretend to be one. But he didn't begin
like that.

8

The Soul's Destroyer

The first edition of *The Soul's Destroyer* was published in 1907, and reprinted in the following year and then again in 1910. These were the poems Davies himself chose. They were the poems he wished to test on the public. And the public wanted more. But, as we have seen from Thomas's selection from Davies's second book, readers preferred 'Nature' poems to poems about the seedier and sordid aspects of human existence. The book is now an expensive collector's item, and extremely rare, but all of the poems can be recovered from the *Complete Poems* of 1963. They range from 'Autumn', on page 23, to 'The Soul's Destroyer' which begins on page 41 and finishes on page 52.

It's a strong collection and one is not surprised that it made the impact it did. There are weaknesses, but they are less common than in Davies's subsequent collections: 'A Drinking Song' (in spite of its title), 'Death', 'The Prover', 'Love's Coming', and 'Lines to a Sparrow'. But there are also poems which rank among the best of Davies: 'Autumn' (a 'Nature' poem which is saved from bathos by Davies's poetic assurance), 'Love Absent', 'Saints and Lodgers', 'In a Lodging House', 'The Hillside Park', and the superb 'The Lodging House Fire'.

'The Hillside Park' is extraordinary. Here is a poem which Davies could so easily have ruined by sentimental caprice and quaint artifice, but instead he controls it with great assurance and immense technical skill in an almost faultless imitation of the eighteenth-century pastoral style:

> Without a branch of wood
> Plants, giant-leaved, like boneless bodies stood.
> The flowers had colonies, not one was seen
> To go astray from its allotted green,
> But to the light like mermaids' faces came
> From waves of green, and scarce two greens the same.
> And everywhere man's ingenuity
> On fence and bordering: for I could see
> The tiny scaffolding to hold the heads
> And faces overgrown of flowers in beds
> On which their weak-developed frames must fall,
> Had they not such support upright and tall.

There is a nice particularity in all this, and an understated descriptive accuracy: Davies could, when he wished, do this kind of thing, and it fitted well the poems which describe, with unflinching accuracy, the miseries and despair of the lodging houses and backstreets with which Davies was familiar:

> ... when old Thames rolls in his fog, and men
> Are lost, and only blind men know their way;
> When Morning borrows of the Evening's lamps,
> Or when bewildered millions battle home
> With stifled throats, and eyes that burn with pain..

... in thy slums, where I have seen men gaunt,
In their vile prisons where they wander starved
Without a jailer for their common needs ...

Nothing even remotely Georgian about all that, and in technically competent blank verse, too. So, why did generations of editors, readers, reviewers, critics and those who should have known better make so little of this other, more powerful side of Davies? Well, for whatever reasons, they did, and Davies's reputation has suffered badly in consequence.

Roy Campbell summed up the six qualities which were 'a safe passport to half a dozen anthologies', and he was speaking of Georgian anthologies. To quote them:

1. Have you ever been on a walking tour?
2. Do you suffer from Elephantiasis of the Soul?
3. Do you make friends easily with dogs, poultry, etc?
4. Are you easily exalted by natural objects?
5. Can you write in rhyme and metre?

Poor Davies had all the necessary qualifications, and necessity as well as opportunism caused him to exercise them. But he had so much more than that and, in his heart of hearts, he knew it.

Davies's apprenticeship was based on an instinctive appreciation of the poems of Herrick and Burns. His taste was for the lyric poems which were at the heart of Elizabethan poetry, when the language was fresh and emotion found musical expression. His anthology *Jewels of Song*, published by Cape in 1930, epitomises his poetic taste. As he says in his Introduction, 'the reader can open the book at any page and find a thing of beauty, and be free of doubt'. And it is that last phrase which gives the game away. True poems were, to Davies, obviously so.

This is, by any account, an excellent anthology. It includes a substantial number of anonymous lyrics which are an established part of the English poetic tradition, as well as poems which have legitimately become familiar to all those readers who take a serious interest in English poetry. But there are also poems here which will be unfamiliar and are, perhaps, of dubious merit: poems by Lascelles Abercrombie, Humbert Wolfe, Herbert Palmer, and Charles Dalmon, for example. These are poets who were his contemporaries and whom Davies claims to have judged by the standards 'of my own work'. And yet the poems of his own that Davies includes are the much anthologised 'Leisure' and 'The Kingfisher'. He claims that the poems of his contemporaries which he has chosen are poems he himself is 'jealous of and would be glad of the chance of stealing'. Really? What about this (by Padraic Colum):

> I heard in the night the pigeons
> Stirring within their nest;
> The wild pigeon's stir was tender,
> Like a child's hand at the breast.
>
> I cried, 'O stir no more!
> (My breast was touched of tears),
> O pigeons, make no stir –
> A childless woman hears.'

The poems a poet chooses to anthologise not only give a clue to the strengths and weaknesses of a poet's taste but also to the flaws in his or her own work. A good example is Yeats's *Oxford Book of Modern Verse*, published in 1936, which many found inconsistent with the kind of poet they felt he had become. But Yeats changed, Davies didn't.

In his Introduction, Davies says, emphatically, that anthologies 'have now become something of a pest' but he excuses this one by saying that he wanted to bring together poems of less than twenty-four lines which were 'little masterpieces'. He says he has judged the poems 'by no other than my own work and, in the case of contemporary poems, 'only those that I am jealous of.'

The selection is interesting because of its breadth and eclecticism. There are poems by Matthew Arnold, William Blake, Robert Browning, Robert Burns, Byron, Thomas Campion, Chaucer, Coleridge, Cowley, Crashaw, Sir John Davies, Dekker, Donne, Drayton, Hardy, Herbert, Herrick, Jonson, Keats, Landor, Marlowe, Marvell, Milton, Raleigh, Christina Rossetti, Shakespeare, Shelley, Sidney, Suckling, Tennyson, Waller, Wordsworth, and Yeats. And that's not mentioning all of the well-known names Davies includes from the history of English verse.

Other, lesser-known poets, are there, too: Anna Laetitia Barbauld (1743-1925), Richard Barnfield (1574-1637), Barnabe Barnes (1569-1624), Aphra Benn (1640-1689), Charles Best (17th Century), Richard Doddridge Blackmore (1825-1900), Nicholas Breton (1545-1626) – to give only a sample.

So too, of course, are the popular poets of his day: Abercrombie, A.E., Belloc, Binyon, Bridges, Brooke, Church, Joseph Campbell, Padraic Colum, Charles Dalmon, de la Mare, Eleanor Farjeon, Graves, Gurney, Hodgson, Masefield, Sturge Moore, Morgan, Seamus O'Sullivan, Herbert Palmer, Siegfried Sassoon, James Stephens, and Humbert Wolfe (and so many of these are now forgotten or unread). But most of the poems he chose, irrespective of who they were by, possess a poetic quality that Davies himself instinctively felt to be intrinsically poetic. Apart from anonymous songs, the largest contributors are Blake, Campion, Herrick, Shakespeare, and Wordsworth. These were the poets from whom Davies learnt the most, and the ones he emulated.

There are gems here, and there are duds, with the duds more common among the choices from his contemporaries. To choose poems by contemporaries is not only to be hampered by the ties of friendship, even literary acquaintance, but also to be blinded by the force of contemporary fashion and prejudice. So, from Yeats, Davies chooses 'When You Are Old', 'A Faery Song', and 'The Lake Isle of Innisfree' rather than the poems which were beginning to define a more modern, less romantic poet. Many of Davies's own poems would fit nicely into this choice of contemporary poems.

Fortunately, it was the older poets who defined the style and manner that Davies mostly had recourse to: the Blake of 'Tyger', the 'Cherry Ripe' of Campion (which could almost have been written by Davies himself), the 'To Dianeme' of Herrick, the 'Sigh no more, Ladies, sigh no more' of Shakespeare, and Wordworth's 'The Daffodils'. Davies's imitation of these models was extaordinarily close but what, I think, he was after was the 'frisson' which they achieved: that nerve-touching magic which sparked the whole.

Mostly, he failed, as one would expect. And he didn't have the courage (and could not afford) to discard those poems which he must have known failed to ignite. Because there was no sympathetic reader around to encourage him to do otherwise, he turned out poem after poem to suit current tastes. He might have done otherwise, but it would be unfair to castigate him. He was, as we all are to a greater or lesser extent, the victim of contemporary fashion.

The Complete Poems of W.H. Davies is a weighty volume, even in paperback. Its size is daunting, and the arrangement of the poems can be confusing. Initially, the order of the poems follows the order in the collections where the poems were first published, the collections themselves being printed sequentially throughout. But there are maddening exceptions: eighteen of the poems from *New Poems* (1907) are printed between pages 500 and 600, instead of being with the poems which begin on page 52. *Nature Poems* (1908) begins on page 75, but some of the poems are printed, again, between pages 500 and 600. The problem continues throughout the book and, as far as I know, no attempt has been made so far to break the whole body of Davies's poems into separate sections, clearly demarcated, within a single volume.

The titles and dates of the separate collections are as follows:

The Soul's Destroyer (Alston Rivers, 1907)
New Poems (Elkin Matthews, 1907)
Nature Poems and Others (Fifield, 1908)
Farewell to Poesy and Other Pieces (Fifield, 1910)
Songs of Joy and Others (Fifield, 1911)
Foliage: Various Poems (Elkin Matthews, 1913)
The Bird of Paradise and Other Poems (Methuen, 1914)
Child Lovers and Other Poems (Fifield, 1916)
Forty New Poems (Fifield, 1918)

The Song of Life and Other Poems (Fifield, 1920)
The Hour of Magic and Other Poems (Cape, 1922)
Secrets (Cape, 1924)
A Poet's Alphabet (Cape, 1925)
The Song of Love (Cape, 1926)
A Poet's Calendar (Cape, 1927)
Ambition and Other Poems (Cape, 1929)
Poems 1930–1931 (Cape, 1931)
My Birds (Cape, 1933)
Love Poems (Cape, 1933)
The Birth of Song (Cape, 1936)
The Loneliest Mountain and Other Poems (Cape, 1939)

Such a long list of poetry collections published at such regular intervals, with little more than a year or so between books, suggests a poet who was too keen to satisfy his publishers and readers and too keen to remain continuously in print. No poet who believed, as Davies most surely did, in the fresh inspiration or impulse which necessitated the birth of a poem could have produced verse so consistently in such bulk. The sheer quantity of poems begins to look like production to order. It is a corpus which demands to be slimmed down to its essentials.

9

The Essential Davies

The *Complete Poems*, published by Jonathan Cape in 1963, contains 749 poems, most of them short lyrics. No poet could be expected to produce that number of poems without sacrificing quality to quantity. Davies who, apart from a small pension, had no other means of livelihood and was determined to avoid paid employment of any kind, produced volume after volume of poetry to satisfy the market for his work. His income was small, but it was reasonably constant. He complained, of course, that his poems did not make him a rich man, but that was Davies all over. What such production did do, however, was make him into the kind of poet his publishers wanted him to be, rather than the kind of poet he essentially was. The poet of 'Leisure' celebrated in anthology after anthology disguises a poet who, at his best, produced a significant number of poems which deserve to survive the vagaries of fashion.

He was, at one time, at the heart of poetic fashion. His poems appeared in all of the five volumes of *Georgian Poetry* published between 1911 and 1922, and these volumes had a huge circulation. They defined, for the ordinary reader, what poetry actually was, and they secured Davies's reputation as an essential member of a small, but significant, literary elite. But, as what became known as 'Georgian Poetry' lost its interest for the reading public, especially after the First World War, Davies's reputation, as a significant 'Georgian', suffered.

Unlike a few other poets who had once belonged to the Georgian fold, Davies never changed. He remained more or less the kind of poet he had always been. Graves did change, and so did Lawrence, and Walter de la Mare (of whom Davies was extremely jealous, perhaps realising how good he was) had technical and intellectual gifts which were beyond Davies and which were much admired by Eliot and Leavis. But while Graves worked out his poetic future in Mallorca, and Lawrence's restlessness found some respite in the Mediterranean, Australia, and Mexico, Davies retired to Gloucestershire and his cottage garden. But there remained, and still remains, a vein of gold which runs right through the hefty *Complete Poems*. The problem is to find it, and to establish the poems which belong to it.

So, where is the true Davies? It would be unfair to expect a reader to plough through the 749 poems of the *Complete Poems* to find him, and the earlier *Collected Poems* of 1940 is fast becoming as rare as those of 1923, 1928, and 1934, all of which are practically unavailable. There was a *Selected Poems* in 1923, and 1928, but these, too, are very rare. Perhaps the Faber selection *Common Joys and Other Poems* might be worth looking for, but the more obvious choice would be Jonathan Barker's *W.H. Davies: Selected Poems*, published by OUP in 1985. However, that too has long been out of print, and is difficult to find. But it did, with some success, try to identify a different Davies from the one readers had become used to.

One of the most anthologised of W.H. Davies's poems has been the poem 'Leisure'. This first appeared in *Songs of Joy and Others*, published by Fifield in 1911. Here it is, in full:

> What is this life if, full of care,
> We have no time to stand and stare.
>
> No time to stand beneath the boughs
> And stare as long as sheep or cows.
>
> No time to see, when woods we pass,
> Where squirrels hide their nuts in grass.
>
> No time to see in broad daylight,
> Streams full of stars like skies at night.
>
> No time to turn at Beauty's glance,
> And watch her feet, how they can dance.
>
> No time to wait till her mouth can
> Enrich that smile her eyes began.
>
> A poor life this if, full of care,
> We have no time to stand and stare.

The first thing to notice about the poem is the lack of detail. Davies is writing about having time to notice the things around us, not in the city or town but in the country. No birds are mentioned, no trees are named, and no plants, except for grass. The only animals mentioned are sheep and cows, and squirrels.

No attempt is made to describe these creatures, although we are reminded that sheep and cows stare, and that squirrels hide their nuts, although we are not told what kind of nuts these might be. The poem, in fact, was written by someone who was, essentially, a townsman. In his descriptions of his travels through much of the United States, Davies almost never made any attempt to describe the countryside he passed through, and the same went for his journeying through parts of England and Wales. Davies, like today's town or city dweller, escaped to the country from time to time, as a relief from the stress and noise of urban living. He always dreamt of living in the country, and that's where the later part of his life was spent, but he was never, really, a countryman.

The observation that a stream with the sunlight flashing and sparkling on it can seem like a night sky full of stars is a far-fetched simile and distanced from exact experience. And then, in the closing lines of the poem we are encouraged to lose ourselves in an abstraction, 'Beauty', who is personified as a smiling and dancing woman, before the poem culminates in an echo of the first two lines.

Rhythmically, the poem is very simple, consisting of rhymed couplets with four equal stresses per line. There is no play with this, no variation, except in the line 'Streams full of stars like skies at night'.

We can fruitfully compare this poem with a poem by the Northamptonshire poet, John Clare, who died in 1864. Clare really *was* a countryman, and knew what he was talking about. His poems, although every bit as emotionally charged as Davies's, are filled out with the detail of the natural world. Take, for example, his poem entitled 'The Thrush's Nest':

> Between a thick and spreading hawthorn bush
> That overhung a molehill large and round
> I heard from morn to morn a merry thrush
> Sing hymns to sunrise while I drank the sound.
> With joy and often an intruding guest
> I watched her secret toils from day to day.
> How true she warped the moss to form her nest
> And modelled it within with wood and clay.
> And bye and bye like heath bells gilt with dew
> There lay her shining eggs as bright as flowers
> Ink-spotted over shells of greeny blue.
> And there I witnessed in the summer hours
> A brood of nature's minstrels chirp and fly
> Glad as the sunshine and the laughing sky.

Whether or not Davies ever saw a thrush's nest, he certainly didn't write about it. He did write a poem entitled 'A Young Thrush', but there is nothing in the poem that distinguishes his thrush from other birds. Clare wrote about snipes, sand martins, wrens, wrynecks, yellowhammers and many other birds he was familiar with, often using local names for them. Davies, however, wasn't really interested in birds other than the familiar blackbird, sparrow, skylark, and so on. In his much-anthologised 'The Kingfisher', he writes about a bird which has a particularly vivid plumage, which makes Davies think of rainbows and peacocks, of green parks and lawns and then, in a final stanza, states that this bird has 'no proud, ambitious mind'. Although the poem encourages us to recall our own experiences of seeing a kingfisher 'away from all mankind', perhaps by 'a lonely pool' when we were sitting under an overhanging tree, the poem falsifies the experience by asserting that this bird has no ambitions of clapping its wings 'before the windows of proud kings'. When Clare writes about birds he is interested in them as birds, not as excuses for projecting onto them thoughts and feelings which birds don't have. Davies's sparrows are 'feathered bullies' who 'roll fighting in wet mud' and should, instead, look at the linnets who 'like ladies sing'. Clare's sparrows, on the other hand, are hedge sparrows with their own specific plumage, nesting habits, and eggs.

Notice, in Clare's poem, how the thrush's nest is built in a specific bush, the hawthorn, and situated in a specific place: the hawthorn which overhung a molehill. Clare is a careful observer who watched the bird build its nest with moss, wood, and clay. The bird 'warped the moss to form her nest'. When Clare saw the eggs in the nest, 'ink-spotted over shells of greeny blue', he was reminded of harebells on the green heathland around the village where he lived. The dew on the eggs was like the dew on those wild flowers. The fledglings are 'a brood of nature's minstrels', chirping and flying in 'the sunshine and the laughing sky'. Clare actually involves us in the detailed experience of finding the nest, seeing how carefully and beautifully it is built, seeing the distinctive eggs of the thrush, and enjoying the small birds' noisy activity in the summer sunshine. Clare is a careful observer of nature, whereas Davies projects onto nature his own human preoccupations, prejudices, and emotions.

But (and this is an important qualification) Davies's preoccupations, prejudices, and emotions as a human being are what, in the end, make his best poems valuable and interesting, and give them the permanence which they deserve. Davies was a complicated human being who lived a difficult and emotionally turbulent life. His moods were often dark, his anxieties (and, indeed, terrors) were real, and his passions were strong. He had lived for much of his life amongst beggars and outcasts, in a hostile and often violent environment, living by his wits and struggling to survive, both physically and mentally. When all this gets into his poems, they have a power and depth which stirs and disturbs us. They are poems of the city. They are poems of despair, courage, passionate engagement, and compassion born of the bitterness of personal experience. His country poems, on the other hand, are poems of escape and relief from the emotional scars which life had inflicted on him. In contrast to poems like 'Leisure' and 'The Kingfisher', let's consider 'Night Wanderers':

> They hear the bell of midnight toll,
> And shiver in their flesh and soul;
> They lie on hard, cold wood or stone,
> Iron, and ache in every bone;
> They hate the night: they see no eyes
> Of loved ones in the starlit skies.
> They see the cold, dark water near;
> They dare not take long looks for fear
> They'll fall like those poor birds that see
> A snake's eyes staring at their tree.
> Some of them laugh, half-mad; and some
> All through the chilly night are dumb;
> Like poor, weak infants some converse,
> And cough like giants, deep and hoarse.

This is poetry of exact statement, spare diction, and fine technical and emotional control. Notice the nice overlap of lines three and four, and lines eleven and twelve, beautifully controlled.

The poem is, of course, a sonnet; but not ostentatiously so. The poet writes easily and naturally within this complex form and his rhymes are unforced and in tune with what he is saying. There are two off-rhymes ('toll/soul' and 'converse/hoarse') which work perfectly and are quite unstrained. The colloquial contraction ('They'll') is part of the poem's intimacy and directness.

There are few adjectives, and none of them is forced: the night is starlit, the water is cold and dark, the men take long looks at it, the night is chilly and the men are dumb. Then, when the intensity of expression forces emotional adjectives, they are resonant with the human sympathy which the poem has engendered: 'like poor, weak infants some converse', succeeded by the powerful last line 'And cough like giants, deep and hoarse'. This is superb poetry, by a master of the art, and there are others like it, and equally as good.

Davies was haunted. He describes the terrors he suffered from vividly in his poem 'The Hermit':

> What moves this man is when the blind bat taps
> His window when he sits alone at night;
> Or when the small bird sounds like some great beast
> Among the dead, dry leaves so frail and light;
>
> Or when the moths on his night-pillow beat
> Such heavy blows he fears they'll break his bones;
> Or when a mouse inside the papered walls,
> Comes like a tiger crunching through the stones.

'This man' is Davies himself, and he meant every word of this poem. This is the man we should look for in his poems, rather than be distracted by the poems he wrote to please his publishers, to woo an admiring public, or to earn his bread and butter. I think Davies knew which of his poems were the real thing and which were fakes, and I think he knew that after his death the best of them would survive. It's not easy to find them within the density of the *Complete Poems*, but they are there nevertheless and it is up to discerning readers to discover them for themselves, although I have given suggestions throughout and at the end of this book.

10

Conclusions

Edward Thomas, who was kind and generous to Davies from the start and who found the poet a cottage in Kent to live in shortly after the publication of *The Soul's Destroyer*, wrote glowingly of Davies's poems and became a close friend. But he, too, must bear some of the credit for the public's distorted view of Davies. Most of the poems from *New Poems* (1907) which Thomas particularly praised are true to the Davies of the anthologies, and five of them are, unfortunately, included in Jonathan Barker's *W.H. Davies: Selected Poems*, published by OUP in 1985 and the best selection of the poet made to date, although this selection has been long out of print.

As an example, take 'The Ways of Time':

> As butterflies are but winged flowers,
>   Half sorry for their change, who fain,
> So still and long they lie on leaves,
>   Would be thought flowers again –

E'en so my thoughts, that should expand,
   And grow to higher themes above,
Return like butterflies to lie
   On the old things I love.

If we are to believe, with Richard Stonesifer, that Davies's poetry is 'above all else the reflection of a spirit of inner contentment gained from nature', then this will do very well. But others have been more perceptive. Robert Graves thought him the best poet of his generation and in his Clark Lectures quoted 'The Inquest' – which is included in Jonathan Barker's selection – as an example of the true Davies. In this poem there are none of the common weaknesses evident in 'The Ways of Time': archaic diction, a very generalized and vague impression of the passiveness of the natural world, sentimentality, and commonplace thought. Instead, one notices the absence of archaisms, the concentration and economy, the clever use of colloquial speech and, above all, the originality of conception. The poem shows, too, Davies's characteristic interest in the macabre and the paradoxical:

'Now Gentlemen of the Jury,' said
   The coroner – 'this woman's child
By misadventure met its death.'
   'Aye, aye,' said we. The mother smiled.

And I could see that child's one eye
   Which seemed to laugh, and say with glee:
'What caused my death you'll never know –
   Perhaps my mother murdered me.'

'Poor Davies,' wrote D.H. Lawrence to Edward Marsh, 'he makes me so furious, and so sorry. He's really like a linnet that's got a wee little sweet song, but it only sings when it's wild'. Lawrence wished that one might be cruel enough to drive him to 'leave his Sevenoaks room, where he is rigged up as a rural poet, proud of his gilt mirror and his romantic past'. And, apart from the reference to the 'wee little sweet song', Lawrence was right. By 1913, when this letter was written, Davies was at the height of his fame. He had met most of the famous literary men of the day: in addition to Edward Thomas, he knew Walter de la Mare, Hilaire Belloc, John Galsworthy, Joseph Conrad and John Masefield, among others. There seems to be practically no-one of any reputation in the literary world of the time whom he did not encounter.

Some of these encounters are recorded in *Later Days* which, as I have suggested, might be considered a tired, rather conceited collection of trivial and commonplace reminiscences. The paperback reprint, published in the same year as Jonathan Barker's selection of poems, did nothing to clarify Davies's true status. As I said earlier, the book has almost nothing of the plainness and authenticity of *The Autobiography of a Super Tramp*. Here was Davies, the establishment figure, confessing how little he enjoyed literary company, but compelled by vanity to seek it. Edward Thomas – though he did bear some responsibility for Davies's position – had been well aware of the danger of Davies's writing and publishing too much and had, at the outset of Davies's career, warned him of this danger. But Davies was vain, and not to be restrained. Far too many of his poems – and prose books like *Later Days*, written when he was fifty-four – are unfortunate examples of Davies's lack of self-discipline. He was too easily satisfied and doggedly prolific.

To restore the balance in favour of the poet of 'The Inquest' rather than the poet of 'The Ways of Time', it is necessary to concentrate on the poems which are most free of what one might call 'de la Mare diction' since, although Davies was jealous of his contemporary, he was certainly much influenced by him. Davies gives himself away in the poem 'Confession' – which is in Jonathan Barker's selection – when he says:

> ... [and] in my ninety hours and nine
> I would not tell what thoughts are mine:
> They're not so pure as find their words
> In songs of childhood, flowers and birds.

Though other poems like this are included in Jonathan Barker's selection, which was intended 'to aid a proper evaluation of the poet', they tend to be swamped by far too many poems of the kind that made Davies one of the most popular of the Georgians. The selection – more than one third of Davies's poetic output is included – is much too generous.

It is those very 'songs of childhood, flowers and birds' which provide the bulk of Davies's *Complete Poems*, and on which his reputation used to rest. Because of this, he is a poet who is now rarely read. I do not mean to imply that all such poems are worthless. This is by no means the case. What I do suggest is that Davies's true standing as a poet should be based on those poems which none of his Georgian contemporaries could have written, and which, like few of theirs, have continuing relevance. To make an interesting comparison, Andrew Young – never one of the Georgians – published his first book in 1920, by which time Davies, only fourteen years Young's senior, had already published twelve books, including a *Collected Poems*. Yet, whereas Andrew Young has steadily accumulated a reputation and readership based on his true worth, Davies rapidly acquired a fame which he has as rapidly lost – a fame based on those poems most acceptable to the literary fashion of the time. Hence, when the fashion changed Davies's reputation went with it. His significance has been obscured by the superficialities of literary publicity. It is time, therefore, to reassess his significance on the basis of those poems which form an enduring body of original work. And this process entails, initially, diverting concentration from the lyrical nature pieces to what the *Atheneum* of 16 March 1907, disparagingly called 'the squalor and sordid realities of life'. Davies, indisputably, knew more than most – and as much as, say, Villon and Baudelaire – what these were.

As he himself says of the poem 'Come Away Death', on page 60 of *Later Days*:

> Now if I sent this poem to an editor it would probably be returned, and another, whose subject was a butterfly or bird, a daisy or a tree, would be accepted. The reason for this is that I have been labelled as a Nature poet, whom the deeper problems of life do not concern.

(Jonathan Barker, incidentally, does not include this poem in his selection.) Because I do not believe Davies to be at all important as a 'Nature poet', I myself would isolate only 'Nailsworth Hill' and 'The Hour of Magic' in Barker's selection as felicitous examples, and for what I can only call their 'magical' quality: something akin to the effect de la Mare achieves so often.

One must not make extravagant claims for Davies. He has

nothing of the technical virtuosity of de la Mare, nothing of the learning and sense of tradition of Blunden, nothing of the careful seriousness of Edward Thomas. The greater part of his work is, as I have suggested, commonplace. There are, however, enough original poems to constitute an important and significant contribution to English poetry. Though Davies is rough in comparison with Herrick, for example, he has much more to say, and it is for the genuine originality of his content that we should respect his best work. In spite of some clumsiness, some banality – even in his better poems, sometimes – Davies could be witty and incisive, as well as extraordinarily fluent.

I would suggest as being of central importance such poems as: 'The Inquest', 'The Hospital Waiting-Room', 'The Lodging House Fire', 'Night Wanderers', 'The Hermit', 'A Chant', 'My Old Acquaintance', and 'The Idiot and the Child'. Not all of them are entirely satisfactory as poems, but they are very obviously Davies's and no one else's. They help to form, as it were, a kernel from which to begin a fresh approach to the poet. They are all based on authentic, first-hand experience – experience which must have done much to determine Davies's characteristic view of life. They give us insights into the singularly odd and totally original way in which he viewed the queer, paradoxical, mysterious, and often malevolent, injustices of this world. They help us to understand his genuine fear, his morbidity, his anxiety, his anger, and his sudden surprise and delight.

There is much in Davies (more evident in his prose than in his poems) that would immediately put the modern reader off. In *Johnny Walker* he refers to 'niggers' although, in those days, readers were not as sensitive to what we call 'racism' as they are today. Whether Davies himself was racist is questionable. He was certainly tribal, but that is a more complex matter. Richard Stonesifer, in his book on Davies, published in 1963, uses the term 'negro' without self-consciousness. However, we can be forgiven for feeling uneasy when Davies calls Italians 'Dagoes' (page 41), mocks Chinese speech ('Lookee at the big bellies I pickee', page 43) and, on page 64, refers again to 'niggers'.

Davies always makes a distinction between 'true beggars' and those who are prepared to work, even a little, to earn their bread. He scorns such people, even peddlars, since 'it is a sure sign of a country's decline when beggars have to resort to carrying laces, pins, needles, and self-made novelties'. Birmingham, he says, 'has, by her cheap goods, turned many a good downright beggar into a small pedlar, which is a great pity'. He himself is prepared to steal if necessary (see the description in the chapter on 'Stiffs'), and has no shame in begging from 'houses that were inhabited by railway men that received their wages on a Friday night'.

He also scorns 'the workhouse tramp' (men who were prepared to accept poor food and a night's bed in the workhouse in return for breaking stones or similar work). Such men, Davies says, have 'not only become a pest to the ratepayers of our country – who support so many workhouses – but has also brought the true beggar to his wit's end to earn a livelihood'. He complains, too, about Salvation Army workers who, by collecting in particular streets, spoil it for beggars.

There are other puzzles, too. Davies was well known for his love of animals and, more than once in *Johnny Walker*, mentions his love of dogs, at the same time aware of the fact that large guard dogs could be very dangerous (see the incident he describes in the chapter 'The Simple Life'). But how do we interpret the story of 'Mr Hog and his fellow Hogs' (in the chapter on 'Stiffs'). This wild pig gets caught by surprise when a train comes along the line. Instead of running off the track, the wild pig tries to out-run the train which 'tossed him some twenty or thirty feet in the air, after which he fell lifeless in the swamps'. Davies makes the story into an amusing interval between describing the habits of 'Stiffs', a despicable breed of men who are yet another example of those poor creatures who are prepared to work for a living.

'Navvies', decent working men who are prepared to do hard physical work, are as nothing compared with the 'downrighter'(the true beggar). The navvy is 'a real working-man' and 'rough, uncouth, and ill-mannered'. Davies has no time for him and tells many a story about how he is outwitted by Davies's fellow tramps. The kinds of trick Davies describes with such relish are described with wit and knowing amusement. He is particularly jealous of a beggar who has been far more successful than he has been on the same patch. How had he done it?

> Before we went to our beds for the night this man gave me a letter to read, and in this letter it said that he was one of the strikers at Longford, and that he had a wife and four children to maintain, and ended with a polite and dignified request for assistance. With this letter he did his business, simply handing it to whoever answered the door, with the request that they would take it in and read it. His time was night, when the whole family were at home, probably two or three working sons and the father; and when he could go from door to door without attracting notice.

Davies's comment: 'Who could insult this man with a common penny?'

What are we to make of all this? And what are we to make of a man who, begging at a house in Oxford, has the door opened by a man who has cut his throat with a razor. He is covered in blood and has the razor in his hand. Davies, terrified of being questioned by the police, escapes into the country and has to sleep out in the rain. His comment: 'I hoped with all my heart that he was dead and his soul in hell'.

Reading *Johnny Walker* is an experience which changes for ever any inclination to regard Davies as a sweet, simple, country-loving singer of popular verses. Whatever he was, he was certainly far from that. Davies was arrogant, and fiercely proud of the fact that he had refused to do any kind of manual work for a living. To his way of thinking, a beggar who is prepared to do any kind of work for a bed 'is a timid man, and he feels less shame in being made a slave than a beggar ... but the true English beggar is a Briton that will never be a slave'.

It is as well to remember all this when one comes to eventually read his poems with the kind of thoroughness that they deserve. In *A Poet's Pilgrimage*, the prejudices and harsh opinions are still there. He is scornful of Welsh workers in 'the tin-plate trade'. He writes about one of them: ' ... this rich working man would yet be penniless and starving after being out of work for little more than a month'. He is shocked that 'these common workers in Wales, who pay so little in rent and nothing to educate their children cannot save anything out of two or three hundred pounds a year'. He didn't like the walk from Llanelly to Swansea because 'where there were no people of wealth or culture there was no beauty'.

These are harsh words about working people and, although Davies was always prepared to put his hand in his pocket as a token to the destitute, he did so in a patronising way. He enjoyed the power which his small income gave him, and he regarded himself as superior to the working classes he came across. He saw himself as part of an aristocracy: artists who were free and independent spirits and who had little, if anything, to do with wage-slaves.

His attitude to those who were not what he saw as true Englishmen (even though he himself was Welsh) is as evident here as elsewhere in his writings. He mentions a man who, 'when he told a Welshman or his wife that a certain article would cost four shillings, he would haggle worse than a Jew', and the same shopkeeper 'would deal with that customer as he would with a Jew'. He caricatures Welsh speech, interspersing their English with 'look you', and he describes 'Scotchmen' as 'porridge eaters'.

His opinions are harsh to the point of being, sometimes, primitive and vindictive. Near Neath, he comes across a tombstone inscribed in tribute to a murdered woman. The inscription on the tombstone ends with the statement that 'God has set his mark upon him' ... who was 'THE SAVAGE MURDERER' and 'THE CRY OF BLOOD' would 'assuredly pursue him to a certain and terrible righteous JUDGEMENT'. Davies makes sure the inscription is faithfully recorded, capitals and all, and says 'Amen' three times to himself, in agreement with its warning of terrible retribution.

Arrived in Newport, Davies renews a few old acquaintances and tells the macabre story of a woman he knew who used to

wear a man's soft cap. When he was a boy, he was somewhat
fearful of her but, curious as to why she wore a cap and seeing
that she was asleep, he removes her cap. 'I saw, first to my surprise
and then to my horror, that two curled horns were sticking out
of her head. To make certain that I was not deceived by her hair
taking this strange shape, I felt them, and sure enough the horns
were hard and made of solid bone'. For some reason, he tries to
find the woman again but hears, from neighbours, that she has
died.

The last person Davies sees in Newport is 'a pleasant cheerful-
looking Jew' who had had 'several great disappointments, enough
to drive a man of his tribe to suicide'. Apparently, this man
belonged to a club 'whose members were mostly Gentiles' and,
for three years in succession, in some kind of annual raffle 'won
a leg of pork'. Davies tells the story but, mischievously, makes no
comment.

Near Pontypool, Davies notices some sheep, 'three or four in
number', whose wool was 'black with coal dust, and did not look
very attractive. If all sheep looked like that they would never have
got into poetry or on the painter's canvas'. Strange comment,
but indicative, perhaps, of an attitude which is disappointingly
conventional. In this book, Davies astonishes the reader more
than once by such commonplace reflections. For instance, having
already told us the awful story of the woman with two horns on
her head, he is shocked when he hears a tale told about how an
actor, trying to put off a girl who is in love with him, 'made such
a beast of himself that the girl was throroughly disgusted'. What
did the actor do? He 'made the end of his nose wet with soup; he
used his bare hands both at once to carry the food to his mouth,

and kept blowing his nose in the most objectionable way into his handkerchief'. Davies comments that it is 'a good example of what passes for humour with the lower classes in any country'.

When Davies meets a man on the road who suspects him of being some kind of preacher, Davies assures him that he is, in fact, a poet. They walk together along the road for some time and, eventually, end up at the pub, where Davies buys the man a drink. The man has already told Davies that his wife writes poetry and, pressed by the man, who can neither read nor write, Davies copies a poem from his notebook for the man to take to his wife. The poem, one of Davies's best, is the one beginning 'I am the poet Davies, William / I sin without a blush or blink'. Incidentally, most of the poems which Davies uses from time to time in this book are among his better ones, evidence, if one needed it, that he was well aware of their quality. He was never as naïve as his more innocent readers thought he was.

The kind of unpleasant surprise that Davies from time to time springs on the reader occurs towards the end of this book, in a pub in Bristol. A blind man enters and, not long afterwards, Davies and the landlord are in conversation with the man, who is a regular customer. While they are conversing, a 'negro' (as Davies was wont to call a black man) comes in, and orders a drink. As he drinks, the blind man begins to become uncomfortable and, eventually, leaves, crying 'Antipathy, William. Antipathy, William', and he is followed, shortly afterwards, by the black man, who has finished his beer. Davies, however, stays behind and asks the landlord why the blind man kept saying that. 'But do you think he knew the stranger was a negro?' Davies asks. 'I certainly do,' says the landlord, 'because of the smell.' And Davies elaborates by recalling how white men in the USA were sensitive to the smell of black men. It's uncomfortable reading.

In *Later Days*, Ralph Hodgson (a poet worth looking up) who was, unlike Davies, teetotal but shared Davies's love of pipe tobacco, dogs and other animals, and boxing, disliked Davies's attitude towards 'coloured men.' Hodgson was uncomfortable with what he called Davies's 'prejudice' and told him so, expecting 'fair play' in Davies's judgement of people. Davies's counter-argument, demanding 'fair play for white men' is feeble in comparison. The exchange, once again, reflects badly on Davies's views about such matters.

Apart from Ralph Hodgson, Davies got to know several other literary figures of the time: Joseph Conrad, Walter de la Mare, Edward Garnett, and Rupert Brooke, to name only a few. Conrad was upset when Davies questioned the fact that he had been a ship's captain, and hunted out his papers to prove it. When asked about de la Mare, Davies confessed that he rarely understood what he was talking about and regarded him as something of a mystery. And Davies says nothing about the quality of de la Mare's poems, or Edward Thomas's for that matter, preferring generalities rather than specific criticism. As for Rupert Brooke, of whose reputation Davies seems bitterly jealous, Davies says, 'he was a charming young man' but 'his work shows not the least sign that he would ever become ... a great poet'.

He was right, of course, about Rupert Brooke, but one would have expected him to make much more of Edward Thomas, the poet who, more than any of Davies's literary contemporaries (apart from Shaw, perhaps), did so much for Davies's poetic career. It was Thomas who not only saw that Davies had a roof over his head and supported him when he was in financial difficulties, but who wrote glowing reviews of his poems and made sure that the literary world was aware of Davies's presence. But one looks in vain in *Later Days* for the kind of literary reciprosity one might have expected. And Edward Thomas, of all the so-called 'Georgian Poets', is the one poet, apart perhaps from Walter de la Mare, who remains a significant presence in contemporary poetry.

We must be cautious in our assessment of Davies. In a letter dated 7 May 1917, the American poet Robert Frost (who had encouraged Edward Thomas to write poetry) wrote to Louis Untermeyer: 'Trust you don't see too much in Davies. He's overrated.' Davies himself, of course, had other ideas about his poetic stature.

'When posterity has confirmed this immortality which contemporary critics have conferred on me ... ' he writes and, later, 'I have not worn out the knees of many trousers in my attempt to climb Parnassus. It is not for me to say whether I have secured a small place on its many slopes – I will leave that to others'. This is all somewhat disingenuous, as when he says ' ... in spite of reaching the front rank of living poets at one stride, I cannot say it has brought me much worldly prosperity.' He was never rich but, on the other hand, he was never as poor as he pretended to be. Others were.

There is certainly evidence, albeit in his own words, of his financial generosity towards other tramps and general down-and-outs, but this never amounted to more than a coin or two. But there is no solid evidence that he had much sympathy for writers who, like himself, were struggling to achieve some kind of reputation. He mentions Hudson's 'bitterness' at being 'old and unrecognised' and cites examples of this bitterness in practice. Davies is contemptuous, 'However, Hudson's manners improved when he knew me better, and he used all his influence in getting me a Civil List pension'.

The most extraordinary evidence of a general lack of emotional connection with what was going on at that time, apart from a few rather conventional platitudes, is Davies's reaction to the Great War of 1914-1918. His chapter entitled 'In Time of War' is predominantly given over to a dispute between him and his noisy neighbour, a Belgian prostitute who plays the Marseillaise loudly until the early hours. Davies, amusingly, responds by singing 'Men of Harlech' when she stops, at 4am, and settles down to sleep. This is after Davies has made a complaint to 'The Chief of Police at Scotland Yard'. Davies makes a number of complaints about the difficulties occasioned by the War, and the way it has affected his domestic routines but, apart from an amusing story or two of this kind, there is no real engaged compassion.

He did a small bit. In 'Reading for Charity' he describes how he joined other writers in reading aloud at public meetings to raise money for the War. Much of this concentrates on his initial shyness at reading in public, but 'although people might think that I was a very bad reader they would not be able to say that I was a very bad poet'. And, of course, he wasn't, as several of the poems he chose to head the chapters in *Later Days* show. But whether he chose to read what he considered his best poems at these public gatherings or simply those poems the public expected him to read is another matter. He complains elsewhere about the kind of poet the public expected him to be but there is little evidence that he did much to determine public taste, even in the anthologies he edited. 'Why are people always insisting that I am a popular poet, which I certainly do not want to be,' he writes.

Davies's relations with contemporary artists were easier than his relations with writers, especially poets. He was not in competition with painters like Sickert and Rothenstein and Augustus John, and sculptors like Epstein and Bresco. He was also flattered by their interest in him as a model and engineered things so that he either got their work cheap or as a gift. He became something of a collector. He could never have afforded to pay the full price for their portraits or busts of himself and made much of the fact that they made such a good living in comparison with poets.

Davies is distinctly odd, if not quaint, in his opinions and reflections on life. He says that, although he is not a Christian himself, he is certainly not an atheist. He dislikes the company of atheists 'because they are loud and vulgar' and generally opinionated. So what, one wonders, might be Davies's personal religious beliefs. It turns out that they amount to nothing more than a fairly vague belief in some kind of retributive reincarnation. As with so much of Davies, outside the best of his poems, his opinions and thoughts differ little from the kind of simplifications and generalities common amongst most of the populace. His sentimentality over animals, his belief in simple retributive justice, his tribal loyalties, his belief in freedom from the drudgery of manual work, his enjoyment of ale and pubs, and his appreciation of the open air and the beauties of the countryside – all are, in essence, too simple and commonplace for comment. His descriptions of his wanderings in the United States and Canada contain no memorable descriptions of those countries and their rich and varied landscapes, and there is nothing in his prose, or his poetry for that matter, to compare with the descriptive detail one finds in John Clare. The few differentiated birds, animals, trees and flowers in Davies's prose and poems appear in the same unlocalised landscape.

Something needs to be said on the question of simplicity – which should not be confused with either innocence or naivety. Although Davies often affected simplicity, both in his style and subject matter, he was no innocent. He often uses the innocence and vulnerability of childhood, for example, as a contrast to the callousness and evil of the adult world. Blake did the same. In these times of hardened sensibility and sophistication on the one hand, and gross sentimentality on the other, few modern poets dare treat of such subjects. It is a sign of Davies's quality that he could, and did, write poems like 'The Little Ones' and 'The Child Chatters'.

Finally, there are the poems where Davies writes of his own predicament. With their tragic stoicism, they are direct and affecting. Davies knew where he had failed and he knew his weaknesses. Now and again, in poems like 'Passion's Hounds', 'Wild Oats', 'Ambition', and 'Friends', Davies writes of his plight with powerful clarity. It is the stoicism of the pagan, with a touch of Hardy in it, and the issues are faced with the same uncompromising courage.

Davies knew the difference between poetry and prose and never confused them. At his best, as in 'Sheep', he was inimitable. Surprisingly, he called himself in one of his poems, 'a poet full of blackest evil', which is something of a counterbalance, though an attractive exaggeration. Certainly, he knew what the word meant. At times, he could express complex ideas with extraordinary eloquence, as in 'An Epitaph' and 'In the End' – both of which Jonathan Barker for some reason overlooked. At other times, he could write in an engagingly plain style.

His faults are obvious, but the range of subject matter is impressive. And behind it all is a singularly complex, sensitive man who, for all his insincerities, could write poems as affecting as any of his, now, more illustrious contemporaries. Prior to Jonathan Barker's selection, the most recent selection of Davies's poems had been the 1928 selection, made for the Gregynog Press by Edward Garnett and, until Barker's selection, none of his poems had been in print for many years. One would have hoped that Jonathan Barker's attractively edited and produced paperback might have led to a long overdue revival of interest in this unusual, rewarding, and too long-neglected poet, but it didn't.

Perhaps this short introduction to both his prose and his poetry will send readers back to his work, and encourage younger readers to explore further. Whatever edition of his poetry is discovered and explored, there are fine and durable poems to be found, and the exploration is well worth the effort. W.H. Davies fully deserves his place in the history of English poetry and a full reassessment of his work has long been overdue.

A Short Bibliography
& A Selection of Poems

A Short Bibliography

Richard Stonesifer's *W.H. Davies: A Critical Biography* is an essential introduction to Davies's life and his work. It was published by Cape in 1963. This can be supplemented by two more recent books: *W.H. Davies* by Lawrence Normand (Seren, 2003) and *Time to Stand and Stare* by Barbara Hooper (Peter Owen, 2004). Although both these books draw on material in Stonesifer's critical biography, they contain interesting new biographical material. Their critical evaluation of Davies's work, however, is sacrificed to biographical content. Barbara Hooper does include a useful small selection of Davies's poems, but the selection is distorted by the inclusion of 'Leisure' and 'The Kingfisher'.

For the serious reader there really is no alternative to ploughing through either the *Complete Poems* of 1962 or one of the earlier *Collected Poems*. I have added a selection of poems an interested reader might care to look up first, and which exemplify the Davies I have been at pains to focus on. The selection is not complete, but provides a useful nucleus for further exploration. Davies's prose work is worth looking up, both in libraries, secondhand bookshops, and on the internet. *The Autobiography of a Super Tramp* is republished from time to time, but it is unlikely that the other prose books will be revived.

The poems in both the variously dated *Collected Poems* and the *Complete Poems* are listed alphabetically at the beginning of the collections, and the poems are in more or less chronological order of publication although, as I have already pointed out, there are exceptions. Individual poems are not difficult to find. There is an index of first lines at the end of the collections. The selection I have made follows the order in the *Complete Poems*.

Jonathan Barker, in his *Selected Poems*, usefully groups his selection by dated publication so that the reader can follow the progression from book to book. This is particularly helpful for anyone wishing to study Davies's poetic development, although I personally hold that this is not the best way to evaluate his work. I do not believe that Davies 'developed'. It seems to me that he tended to lose contact with what I might call his 'best poetic self' as he got older and more anthologised. But readers must make up their own minds about this.

The selection of poems which follows represents, for me, the true Davies. They are poems which no one else, to my knowledge, could have written; and they bear the unmistakable imprint of a man whose sensibility was shaped by the grim experiences of his earlier life. All these poems have what you might call 'bite', and their fat has been trimmed off. The taste is unmistakable Davies. It's an acquired taste, admittedly, but the effort, once made, will help the reader to find other poems from his dense output which measure up to those I have chosen.

Many years ago, I prepared a selection of Davies's poems for Carcanet, and all of the poems I have selected here would have been included. Unfortunately, a selection of his poems was already in preparation (the OUP selection by Jonathan Barker) with consequential copyright problems, so the idea had to be abandoned. However, I was able to use most of my introductory material in a review of Barker's selection in *PN Review*. Some of this material has been incorporated into this book and I am grateful to Michael Schmidt, of Carcanet, for that distant opportunity to bring W.H. Davies back into focus.

THE LODGING HOUSE FIRE

My birthday – yesterday,
Its hours were twenty-four;
Four hours I lived lukewarm,
And killed a score.

I woke eight times and rose,
Came to our fire below,
Then sat four hours and watched
Its sullen glow.

Then out four hours I walked,
The lukewarm four I live,
And felt no other joy
Than air can give.

My mind durst know no thought
It knew my life too well:
'Twas hell before, behind,
And round me hell.

Back to that fire again,
Ten hours I watch it now,
And take to bed dim eyes,
And fever's brow.

Ten hours I give to sleep,
More than my need, I know;

But I escape my mind
And that fire's glow.

For listen: it is death
To watch that fire's glow;
For, as it burns more red
Men paler grow.

O better in foul room
That's warm, make life away,
Than homeless out of doors,
Cold night and day.

Pile on the coke, make fire,
Rouse its death-dealing glow;
Men are borne dead away
Ere they can know.

I lie; I cannot watch
Its glare from hour to hour;
It makes one sleep, to wake
Out of my power.

I close my eyes and swear
It shall not wield its power;
No use, I wake to find
A murdered hour

Lying between us there!
That fire drowsed me deep,
And I wrought murder's deed –
Did it in sleep.

I count us, thirty men,
Huddled from Winter's blow,
Helpless to move away
From that fire's glow.

So goes my life each day –
Its hours are twenty-four –
Four hours I live lukewarm,
And kill a score.

No man lives life so wise
But unto Time he throws
Morsels to hunger for
At his life's close.

Were all such morsels heaped –
Time greedily devours,
When man sits still – he'd mourn
So few wise hours.

But all my day is waste,
I live a lukewarm four
And make a red coke fire
Poison the score.

THE IDIOT AND THE CHILD

There was a house where an old dame
   Lived with a son, his child and wife;
And with a son of fifty years,
   An idiot all his life.

When others wept this idiot laughed,
   When others laughed he then would weep:
The married pair took oath his eyes
   Did never close in sleep.

Death came that way, and which, think you,
   Fell under that old tyrant's spell?
He breathed upon that little child,
   Who loved her life so well.

This made the idiot chuckle hard:
   The old dame looked at that child dead
And him she loved – 'Ah, well; thank God
   It is no worse!' she said.

SHEEP

When I was once in Baltimore,
   A man came up to me and cried,
'Come, I have eighteen hundred sheep
   And we will sail on Tuesday's tide.

'If you will sail with me, young man,
   I'll pay you fifty shillings down;
These eighteen hundred sheep I take
   From Baltimore to Glasgow town.'

He paid me fifty shillings down,
   I sailed with eighteen hundred sheep;
We soon had cleared the harbour's mouth,
   We soon were in the salt sea deep.

The first night we were out at sea
   Those sheep were quiet in their mind;
The second night they cried with fear –
   They smelt no pastures in the wind.

They sniffed, poor things, for their green field,
   They cried so loud I could not sleep:
For fifty thousand shillings down
   I would not sail again with sheep.

THE LITTLE ONES

The little ones are put in bed,
    And both are laughing, lying down;
Their father, and their mother too,
    Are gone on Christmas eve to town.

'Old Santa Claus will bring a horse,
    Gee up:' cried little Will, with glee;
'If I am good, I'll have a doll
    From Santa Claus' – laughed Emily.

The little ones are gone to sleep,
    Their father and their mother now
Are coming home, with many more –
    They're drunk, and make a merry row.

The little ones on Christmas morn
    Jump up, like skylarks from the grass;
And then they stand as still as stones,
    And just as cold as stones, Alas!

No horse, no doll beside their bed,
    No sadder little ones could be;
'We did some wrong,' said little Will –
    'We must have sinned,' sobbed Emily.

NIGHT WANDERERS

They hear the bell of midnight toll,
And shiver in their flesh and soul;
They lie on hard, cold wood or stone,
Iron, and ache in every bone;
They hate the night: they see no eyes
Of loved ones in the starlit skies.
They see the cold, dark water near;
They dare not take long looks for fear
They'll fall like those poor birds that see
A snake's eyes staring at their tree.
Some of them laugh, half-mad; and some
All through the chilly night are dumb;
Like poor, weak infants some converse,
And cough like giants, deep and hoarse.

THE HERMIT

What moves that lonely man is not the boom
  Of waves that break against the cliff so strong;
Nor roar of thunder, when that travelling voice
  Is caught by rocks that carry far along.

'Tis not the groan of oak tree in its prime,
  When lightning strikes its solid heart to dust;
Nor frozen pond when, melted by the sun,
  It suddenly doth break its sparkling crust.

What moves that man is when the blind bat taps
  His window when he sits alone at night;
Or when the small bird sounds like some great beast
  Among the dead, dry leaves so frail and light;

Or when the moths on his night-pillow beat
  Such heavy blows he fears they'll break his bones;
Or when a mouse inside the papered walls,
  Comes like a tiger crunching through the stones.

IN THE END

With all thy gold, thou canst not make
   Time sell his sand;
With all thy cloth, a thin white shroud
   Is Death's command;
Death gives thee but a poor man's space,
   With all thy land.

The beggar in his grave and thou
   Must be the same;
For neither thou nor he shall hear
   Men's praise or blame;
Though thunder and a thousand rocks
   Should call thy name.

THE HOSPITAL WAITING ROOM

We wait our turn, as still as mice,
For medicine free, and free advice:
Two mothers, and their little girls
So small – each one with flaxen curls –
And I myself, the last to come.
Now as I entered that bare room,
I was not seen or heard; for both
The mothers – one in finest cloth,
With velvet blouse and crocheted lace,
Lips painted red, and powdered face;
The other ragged, whose face took
Its own dull, white, and wormy look –
Exchanged a hard and bitter stare.
And both the children, sitting there,
Taking example from that sight,
Made ugly faces, full of spite.
This woman said, though not a word
From her red painted lips was heard –
'Why have I come to this, to be
In such a slattern's company?'
The ragged woman's look replied –
'If you can dress with so much pride,
Why are you here, so neat and nice,
For medicine free, and free advice?'
And I, who needed richer food,
Not medicine, to help my blood;

Who could have swallowed then a horse,
And chased its rider round the course,
Sat looking on, ashamed, perplexed,
Until a welcome voice cried – 'Next!'

THE INQUEST

I took my oath I would inquire,
    Without affection, hate, or wrath,
Into the death of Ada Wright –
    So help me God! I took that oath.

When I went out to see the corpse,
    The four months' babe that died so young,
I judged it was seven pounds in weight,
    And little more than one foot long.

One eye, that had a yellow lid,
    Was shut – so was the mouth, that smiled;
The left eye open, shining bright –
    It seemed a knowing little child.

For as I looked at that one eye,
    It seemed to laugh, and say with glee:
'What caused my death you'll never know –
    Perhaps my mother murdered me.'

When I went into court again,
    To hear the mother's evidence –
It was a love-child, she explained.
    And smiled, for our intelligence.

'Now, Gentlemen of the Jury,' said
    The coroner – 'this woman's child

By misadventure met its death.'
   'Aye, aye,' said we. The mother smiled.

And I could see that child's one eye
   Which seemed to laugh, and say with glee:
'What caused my death you'll never know –
   Perhaps my mother murdered me.'

FRIENDS

They're creeping on the stairs outside,
  They're whispering soft and low;
Now up, now down, I hear his friends,
  And still they come and go.

The sweat that runs my side, from that
  Hot pit beneath my shoulder,
Is not so cold as he will be,
  Before the night's much older.

My fire I feed with naked hands,
  No sound shall reach their ears;
I'm moving like the careful cat,
  That stalks a rat it fears.

And as his friends still come and go,
  A thoughtful head is mine:
Had Life as many friends as Death,
  Lord, how the world would shine!

And since I'll have so many friends,
  When on my death-bed lying –
I wish my life had more love now,
  And less when I am dying.

CONFESSION

One hour in every hundred hours
I sing of childhood, birds and flowers;
Who reads my character in song
Will not see much in me that's wrong.

But in my ninety hours and nine
I would not tell what thoughts are mine:
They're not so pure as find their words
In songs of childhood, flowers and birds.

MY OLD ACQUAINTANCE

Working her toothless gums till her sharp chin
Could almost reach and touch her sharper nose,
These are the words my old acquaintance said:
'I have four children, all alive and well;
My eldest girl was seventy years in March,
And though when she was born her body was
Covered all over with black hair, and long,
Which when I saw at first made me cry out,
'Take it away, it is a monkey – ugh!'
Yet she's as smooth and fair as any, now.
And I, who sit for hours in this green space
That has seven currents of good air, and pray
At night to Jesus and His Mother, live
In hopes to reach my ninetieth year in June.
But ere it pleases God to take my soul,
I'll sell my fine false teeth, which cost five pounds,
Preserved in water now for twenty years,
For well I know those girls will fight for them
As soon as I am near my death; before
My skin's too cold to feel the feet of flies.
God bless you and good day – I wish you well.
For me, I cannot relish food, or sleep,
Till God sees fit to hold the Kaiser fast,
Stabbed, shot, or hanged – and his black soul
Sent into hell, to bubble, burn and squeal;
Think of the price of fish – and look at bacon!'

PASSION'S HOUNDS

With mighty leaps and bounds,
I followed Passion's hounds,
　　My hot blood had its day;
Lust, Gluttony, and Drink,
I chased to Hell's black brink,
　　Both night and day.

I ate like three strong men,
I drank enough for ten,
　　Each hour must have its glass:
Yes, Drink and Gluttony
Have starved more brains, say I,
　　Than Hunger has.

And now, when I grow old,
And my slow blood is cold,
　　And feeble is my breath –
I'm followed by those hounds,
Whose mighty leaps and bounds
　　Hunt me to death.

A CHANT

With all our mirth, I doubt if we shall be
Like Martha here, in her serenity,
When we're her age; who goes from bed to bed
To wash the faces of the newly dead;
To close their staring eyes and comb their hair,
To cross their hands and change the linen there;
Who helps the midwives to give strength and breath
To babes, by almost beating them to death
With a wet towel; and half drowns them too,
Until their tender flesh is black and blue.
Not all the revels, Martha, we have been to
Can give us, when we're old, a peace like yours –
Due to the corpses you have gone and seen to.

THE HOUR OF MAGIC

This is the hour of magic, when the Moon
   With her bright wand has charmed the tallest tree
To stand stone-still with all his million leaves!
   I feel around me things I cannot see;
I hold my breath, as Nature holds her own.
   And do the mice and birds, the horse and cow,
Sleepless in this deep silence, so intense,
   Believe a miracle has happened now,
And wait to hear a sound they'll recognize,
To prove they still have life with earthly ties?

WILD OATS

How slowly moves the snail, that builds
A silver street so fine and long:
I move as slowly, but I leave
Behind me not one breath of song.
Dumb as a moulting bird am I,
I go to bed when children do,
My ale but two half-pints a day,
And to one woman I am true.
Oh! what a life, how flat and stale –
How dull, monotonous and slow!
Can I sing songs in times so dead –
Are there no more wild oats to sow?

COME AWAY, DEATH

Come away, Death, make no mistake,
   There's no one in the house to die:
She's young and strong, though suffering pain,
   And waits to hear her first-born's cry.

'Nay,' answered Death, 'there's no mistake,
   I've been to this same house before;
Though no one saw a corpse come out,
   Or any mourner at the door.

'I've been to this same house before,
   I know it well from any other:
And now I come again, to see
   A dead-born child destroy its mother.'

AN EPITAPH

Beneath this stone lies one good man; and when
We say his kindly thought towards all men
Was as generous to the living as to the dead –
What more for any mortal could be said?
His only enemies were those he tried
To help, and failed; who blamed him, in their pride,
Forgetting that his power was not as great
As his intention – and their own weak state.
And if he met with men too slow to move
Into the fullness of his own clear love,
He looked for the fault in his own self, and not
Blamed other men – like our more common lot.
His boundless trust and innocence of evil
Tempted the base and mean, and helped the devil.
Since such a man, without suspicion, kind,
Was duped by many a false, ungrateful mind,
He's gone to Heaven – because he lived so well
That many a wretch through him has gone to hell.

AMBITION

I had Ambition, by which sin
    The angels fell;
I climbed and, step by step, O Lord,
    Ascended into Hell.

Returning now to peace and quiet,
    And made more wise,
Let my descent and fall, O Lord,
    Be into Paradise.

NAILSWORTH HILL

The Moon, that peeped as she came up,
  Is clear on top, with all her light;
She rests her chin on Nailsworth Hill,
  And, where she looks, the World is white.

White with her light – or is it Frost,
  Or is it Snow her eyes have seen;
Or is it Cherry blossom there,
  Where no such trees have ever been?

THE CHILD CHATTERS

Good morning to my dolly first,
  Good morning to my cherry tree;
Good morning to my little chicks,
  For them I love to see.

Good morning to my bow-wow-wow;
  Good morning to my bonnet new;
Good morning to my little self,
  To Dad and Mammie too.

Good morning, God which art in Heaven,
  I hope you slept last night quite well;
And please don't vex your head so much
  About the devil in hell.

And if he bothers you too much,
  And you're afraid, and you sleep bad,
Then, God which art in Heaven, you must
  Have whisky, like my Dad.

INDEX

The position of Raymond Chandler in the pantheon of American letters has long been subject to much debate.

Naturally imbued with a literary sensibility Chandler helped to revolutionise the crime genre, bringing to it a colourful, hardedged vernacular allied to a modern social commentary.

Through the figure of private eye Philip Marlowe, Chandler created a contemporary knight errant whose not so picturesque adventures trudging the mean streets of Los Angeles helped to vividly define the moral dilemmas of a dark, uncertain post-war world.

And yet ... can *The Big Sleep, Farewell, My Lovely* and *The Lady in the Lake* be considered 'literature'?

Author Anthony Fowles – who freely admits to writing half-a-dozen 'sub-Chandlerian' thrillers – brings to the discussion both the detached eye of the professional critic and the sympathetic understanding of the practitioner.

It is a background which allows Fowles to make a balanced, finely-nuanced contribution to the ongoing Chandler debate, refusing to relegate the noir master to the wilderness of 'genre writer' but equally avoiding outlandish claims of literary pre-eminence.

In circumventing the pitfalls and simplicities of 'either/or', Fowles places Chandler's achievements in a fully-realised context, enabling the reader to appreciate more deeply the peculiar strengths and limitations of the prose lyricist of the American mid-century.

SWEETLY SINGS DELANEY
A Study of Shelagh Delaney's Work, 1958-68

John Harding

978-1-906075-83-5
204pp

Shelagh Delaney rose to fame following the instant success in 1958 of her first play *A Taste of Honey*. Lauded as Britain's answer to the controversial French novelist Françoise Sagan, Delaney's work scandalised her home city of Salford but established her as one of the country's most original and exhilarating young playwrights during a period in theatre history when women writers were rare and acceptance hard to achieve.

Delaney has served as an inspiration to countless young artists down the succeeding years. Rock star Morrissey wrote, 'She has always been a part of my life as a perfect example of how to get up and get out and do it.' Novelist Jeanette Winterson claimed, 'She was like a lighthouse – pointing the way and warning about the rocks underneath.'

Sweetly Sings Delaney is the story of her first exciting decade as a writer when she not only produced challenging and dramatic work in prose and on stage but also collaborated with some of the most innovative film and documentary-makers of the decade such as Ken Russell, Tony Richardson, Lindsay Anderson, not to mention actor and fellow Salfordian Albert Finney during his first and only foray as a film director.

JOHN KEATS

Against All Doubtings

Andrew Keanie

978-1-906075-75-0 (pbk)
110pp

Having identified him as a sort of semi-educated little cockney chancer, Keats's contemporary reviewers savaged him in the pages of Britain's most influential magazines. High ambition, unaccompanied by high birth, and radical affiliations and liberal inclinations, made him an object of contempt to those of, or aping the opinions of, the literary Establishment. In the short term, he never stood a chance.

Long after his death, his reputation was eventually brightened by much more enthusiastic – if, as some have since argued, misguided – appreciations for his beautiful and powerful otherworldliness.

Later still, in reaction to Keats-lovers' gushing admiration, a much more worldly Keats has been written up – including some bracing insights that seem to owe something to his first reviewers. As Martin Seymour-Smith has said, 'Many privately regard [Keats] with a condescension that is more smug than they would like to admit.'

This largely text-focused study promotes the best energies of a more Romantic view of a key Romantic figure. Keats was inspired and ill. By the time of his death, his genius and tuberculosis had pressurised him into poetry. The best he had to offer – including searching and scintillating confidences concerning how to live one's life in this world of suffering, 'the Vale of Soul-making' – are more accessible to the reader with a taste for poetry than they are to the consumer of ideologically appropriate journalism or ostentatiously unemotional academic analyses.

SECOND WORLD WAR POETRY IN ENGLISH

John Lucas

978-1-906075-78-1 (pbk)
236pp

John Lucas's book sets out to challenge the widely-held assumption that the poetry of the Second World War is, at best, a poor relation to that produced by its predecessor. He argues that the best poetry that came out of the 1939-45 war, while very different from the work of Owen, Rosenberg, Gurney, and their contemporaries, is in no sense inferior. It also has different matters to consider. War in the air, war at sea, war beyond Europe, the politics of Empire, democratic accountability – these are no subjects to be found in the poetry of the Great War. Nor is sex. Nor did American poets have much to say about that war, whereas the Americans Randall Jarrell, Anthony Hecht and Louis Simpson, are among the greatest English-speaking poets of World War Two. Both Hecht and Simpson write about the Holocaust and its aftermath, as do the English poets, Lotte Kramer and Gerda Mayer. For these reasons among others, English-speaking poetry of the Second World War deserves to be valued as work of unique importance.

A.E. HOUSMAN

Spoken and Unspoken Love

Henry Maas

978-1-906075-71-2 (pbk)
978-1-906075-73-6 (hbk)
61pp

A Shropshire Lad by A.E. Housman is one of the best-loved books of poems in English, but even now its author remains a shadowy figure. He maintained an iron reserve about himself – and with good reason. His emotional life was dominated by an unhappy and unrequited love for an Oxford friend. His passion went into his writing, but he could barely hint at its cause. *Spoken and Unspoken Love* discusses all Housman's poetry, especially the effect of an existence deprived of love, as seen in the posthumous work, where the story becomes clear in personal and deeply moving poems.

ERNEST DOWSON

Poetry and Love in the 1890s

Henry Maas

978-1-906075-51-4 (pbk)
978-1-906075-73-6 (hbk)
48pp

Ernest Dowson (1867-1900) is the archetypal poet of the 1890s. His best work comes entirely from the decade, and he died at the end of it.

Steeped in the Latin poets of antiquity and French 19th-century poetry, he developed an individual style which pared down the exuberance of Poe and Swinburne to a classical simplicity marked by meticulous attention to sound and initiating the move to more informal verse, which made his work attractive to the generation of D.H. Lawrence, Pound and Eliot.

His life was archetypal too. Born to respectable wealth and comfort, he was dragged down by family misfortune. His father's business failure and early death, his mother's suicide and his own advancing tuberculosis began the decline. It was hastened by drink and an impossible love for a young girl who never began to understand him.

In the end Dowson, the poet admired by Yeats, Wilde and a host of contemporaries, was reduced to living little better than a tramp in Paris, to die at thirty-two almost a pauper and alcoholic in a London workman's cottage, leaving posterity some of the finest love poetry in English.

BETWEEN TWO WORLDS

A Survey of Writing in Britain, 1900-1914

Hugh Underhill

978-1-906075-55-2 (pbk)
188pp

In 1924 Philip Gibbs, one of the first 'war correspondents' in the modern sense, wrote in his book *Ten Years After: A Reminder*, 'One has to think back to another world in order to see again that year 1914 before the drums of war began to beat. It is a different world now ... ' A certain popular view has persisted of the Edwardian and pre-war Georgian period as a kind of swan-song to a past elegance and grace, and one of pleasure and freedom from anxiety.

The reality, along with, for many, the leisurely pace and settled way of life, was not only one of great intellectual and artistic excitement, but also of unrest, change and controversy. The first section of this survey, 'Britain 1900-1914: Hope, ferment and the abyss', looks at the political, cultural and economic elements of that ferment and the strains evident in British society: the reaction against Victorian attitudes, the pressure for social reform, the campaigns for women's suffrage and Irish Home Rule, the stirrings of Modernism and the move towards social realism in literature and the arts.

Underhill vividly demonstrates how these forces fed into the writing of the period. In the second section of the book, the work of the major authors of the period, Bennett, Wells, Conrad, Forster, Lawrence, Joyce, James, Shaw, Synge, Yeats, Hardy and Edward Thomas, is critically surveyed.

This is followed, in the final section, by a resumé of the work and varying significance of other authors against which those major figures need to be seen.

OTHER TITLES OF INTEREST

STORY
The Heart of the Matter
Maggie Butt (editor)
978-1-871551-93-8 (pbk)   184pp

MATTHEW ARNOLD AND 'THYRSIS'
Patrick Carill Connolly
978-1-871551-61-7 (pbk)   204pp

MILTON'S *PARADISE LOST*
Peter Davies
978-1-906075-47-7 (pbk)   108pp

LIAR! LIAR!
Jack Kerouac – Novelist
R.J. Ellis
978-1-871551-53-2 (pbk)   294pp

JOHN DRYDEN
Anthony Fowles
978-1-871551-58-7 (pbk)   292pp

THE AUTHOR, THE BOOK & THE READER
Robert Giddings
987-1-871551-01-3 (pbk)   240pp

POETRY MASTERCLASS
John Greening
978-1-906075-58-3   142pp

DREAMING OF BABYLON

The Life and Times of Ralph Hodgson

John Harding

978-1-906075-00-2 (pbk)   238pp

WORDSWORTH AND COLERIDGE

Views from the Meticulous to the Sublime

Andrew Keanie

978-1-871551-87-7 (pbk)   206pp

POETRY IN EXILE

A Study of the Poetry of Auden, Brodsky & Szirtes

Michael Murphy

978-1-871551-76-1 (pbk)   270pp

ALEISTER CROWLEY AND THE CULT OF PAN

Paul Newman

978-1-871551-66-2 (pbk)   224pp

IN PURSUIT OF LEWIS CARROLL

Raphael Shaberman

978-1-871551-13-6 (pbk)   146pp

To find out more about these and other titles visit

www.greenex.co.uk